Atlas of the Bible Lands

Edited by HARRY THOMAS FRANK

Professor of Religion
Oberlin College

HAMMOND INCORPORATED   MAPLEWOOD, NEW JERSEY

Title page illustration:
Aerial view of Jerusalem from the east.
Buildings in foreground are on the Mount
of Olives. Beyond is the Dome of the Rock.

Wall painting from tomb at Beni-hasan
depicts Asian people, probably Amorites,
entering Egypt about 1900 B.C.

ATLAS OF THE BIBLE LANDS, New Edition
Entire contents © Copyright 1977, 1984
by HAMMOND INCORPORATED

The maps "Routes in Palestine" and "Economy of
Palestine" on pages 5 and 7 were prepared especially for
Abingdon Press and published in The Interpreter's
Dictionary of the Bible, Supplementary Volume. *They are*
reproduced here with Abingdon's permission.

Library of Congress Cataloging in Publication Data

Hammond Incorporated.
    Atlas of the Bible lands.

    Includes index.
      1. Bible—Geography—Maps.   I. Frank, Harry Thomas.
II. Title.   III. Title: Atlas of the Bible lands.
G2230.H3   1984   912'.33   83-675795
ISBN 0-8437-7056-2 case bound edition
ISBN 0-8437-7055-4 soft cover edition
Printed in the United States of America

Contents

Preface

THE BIBLE is a universal book, restricted neither by time nor place. Over the centuries on all continents its words have carried a message of hope, solace and salvation for the believer, and on the authority of the Holy Word, societies have been shaped and great events set afoot. Moreover, for the individual person of faith, now as in the past, the Bible is both an indispensable guide and a fundamental point of reference.

Yet the events spoken of in the Bible took place at certain times and in definite places. It is, in fact, basic to a Biblical understanding of revelation that its timeless message was given in historical events, through real persons and at places which can be visited by you and by me. The Bible is thus neither a speculative nor a philosophical book. Rather, it is concrete. It offers no essays on the goodness or the near presence of God, but speaks, for instance, of his being with Abraham as he leaves Ur to journey with many adventures and at God's beckoning to Haran, Shechem and Egypt before returning to settle in Beer-sheba (Genesis 11:28-22:19). It was through Moses in "the Wilderness of Sinai" that Israel received the Ten Commandments (Exodus 19-20). God, says the Bible, was present in the struggles of Deborah and her followers ". . . at Taanach, by the waters of Megiddo" (Judges 5:19). And he was revealing himself in the actions of Joseph, who "went up from Galilee, from the city of Nazareth, to Judea, to the city of David, which is called Bethlehem, because he was of the house and lineage of David, to be enrolled with Mary, his betrothed, who was with child" (Luke 2:4-5).

Where are Ur, Haran, Shechem, Egypt, Beer-sheba, the Wilderness of Sinai, Taanach, Megiddo, Galilee, Nazareth, Judea and Bethlehem? Even the casual reader of the Bible will be struck by the frequency and importance of places in the narrative, and no serious student of the Bible can long afford to be without detailed and accurate knowledge of the lands of the Bible. Indeed, from Haran in the north of Syria to Beer-sheba in the south of Israel, Biblical memories haunt almost every ancient site, and once you pass below the towering Lebanon Mountains and the majestic heights of Hermon there is virtually no town or city, no valley, mountain pass or plain which was not the location of some Biblical event.

Consider Paul as he walked northward from Jerusalem, making his way slowly toward Damascus and his startling conversion to Christianity. What places did he pass, and what memories did they hold? We do not know his exact route, but whatever way he went from the Holy City, Biblical memories lay all about him and whispered to him from the soil of the great deeds of God. If Paul went straight north along the mountain ridge, he passed Gibeah within the hour — Gibeah, the home of Saul, first king of Israel — and shortly passed Ramah and Mizpah, both hallowed by Samuel. The next day Paul would ascend slowly as he neared the desolate site of Bethel, which once echoed to Amos' ringing denunciations. Thus along the road through Samaria, following the course of the great Biblical cities that trace that route: Shiloh, Shechem, Samaria, Dothan — and then into and across the Great Plain where Deborah won an astounding victory with the aid of ". . . the onrushing torrent, the torrent Kishon." As the road winds up into the Galilee hills Nazareth lies nestled to the west, and to the east there are the brooding heights of Gilboa on which Saul and Jonathan ". . . swifter than eagles, stronger than lions . . ." had fallen before the Philistines. And so eventually past the Sea of Galilee with all of its associations with Jesus, and up to the Syrian Heights (The Golan) and into Damascus.

Obviously geography alone cannot convey the Biblical message. But geography, history and religion are inseparably bound together in the Bible. Full understanding and a more complete appreciation of the Bible's unique historical revelation depend upon a certain level of knowledge of its physical setting.

With the aid of this completely new edition of *Hammond's Atlas of the Bible Lands*, sites mentioned in the text of both the Old and New Testaments can quickly be located. Journeys — from that of Abraham to those of the early Christian missionaries — can be easily traced, understood and learned. Fresh, up-to-date maps have been combined with evocative photographs and graphic city plans to serve as a readily usable and convenient companion to the study of the Scriptures. Not only does the user of this Atlas gain a sense of the land itself, but because of the large number of concise, uncluttered, historically-oriented maps each Biblical period comes alive. This historical orientation of the maps is aided by the Time Charts which show parallel events at a glance. These charts help the student of the Bible place Biblical events in their larger historical context.

> ". . . the land which you are going over to possess is a land
> of hills and valleys, which drinks water by the rain from
> heaven, a land which the Lord your God cares for; the eyes
> of the Lord your God are always upon it, from the beginning
> of the year to the end of the year."
> — Deuteronomy 11:11-12

HARRY THOMAS FRANK

Physical Map of Palestine

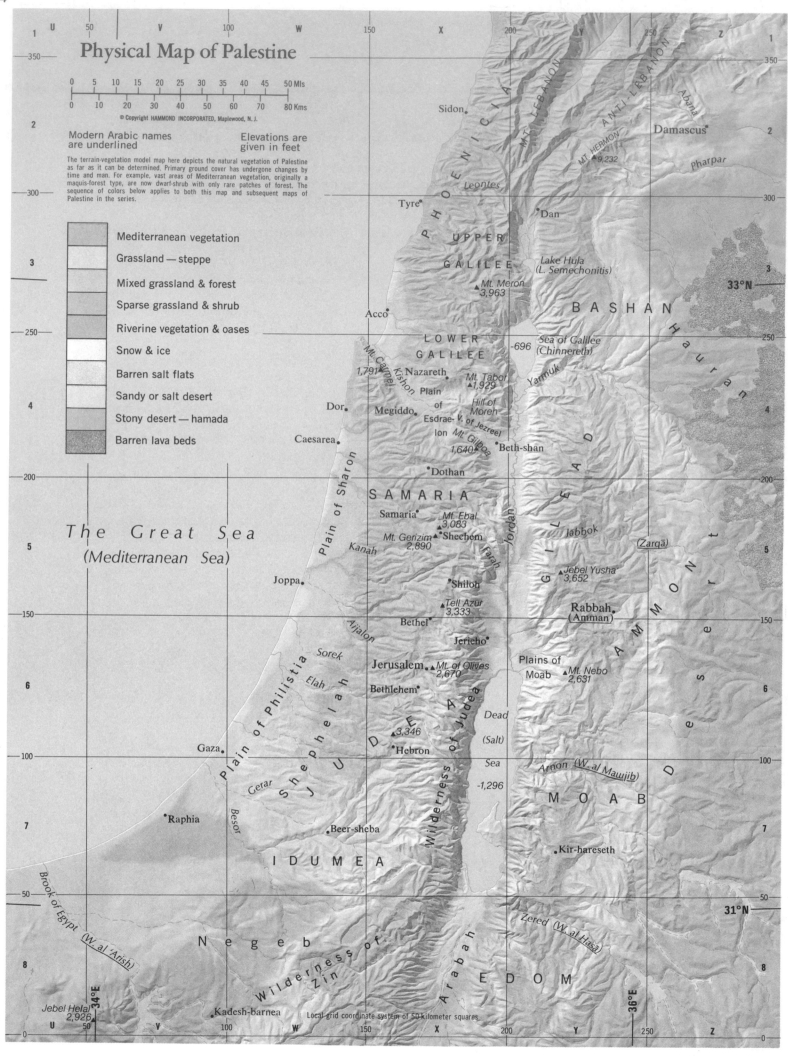

| 0 | 5 | 10 | 15 | 20 | 25 | 30 | 35 | 40 | 45 | 50 Mls |
| 0 | 10 | 20 | 30 | 40 | 50 | 60 | 70 | 80 Kms |

© Copyright HAMMOND INCORPORATED, Maplewood, N.J.

Modern Arabic names
are underlined

Elevations are
given in feet

The terrain-vegetation model map here depicts the natural vegetation of Palestine
as far as it can be determined. Primary ground cover has undergone changes by
time and man. For example, vast areas of Mediterranean vegetation, originally a
maquis-forest type, are now dwarf-shrub with only rare patches of forest. The
sequence of colors below applies to both this map and subsequent maps of
Palestine in the series.

Mediterranean vegetation
Grassland — steppe
Mixed grassland & forest
Sparse grassland & shrub
Riverine vegetation & oases
Snow & ice
Barren salt flats
Sandy or salt desert
Stony desert — hamada
Barren lava beds

The Great Sea
(Mediterranean Sea)

PHOENICIA

Sidon

Tyre

Leontes

Dan

Damascus

MT. LEBANON

ANTI-LEBANON

Abana

Pharpar

MT. HERMON
9,232

33°N

UPPER
GALILEE

Lake Hula
(L. Semechonitis)

BASHAN

Acco

Mt. Meron
3,963

LOWER
GALILEE

-696

Sea of Galilee
(Chinnereth)

Hauran

Mt. Carmel
1,791

Kishon

Nazareth

Mt. Tabor
1,929

Yarmuk

Plain

of

Dor

Megiddo

Esdrae-

Hill of
Moreh

V. of Jezreel

Caesarea

lon

Mt. Gilboa
1,640

Beth-shan

G I L E A D

Dothan

SAMARIA

Plain of Sharon

Samaria

Mt. Ebal
3,083

Mt. Gerizim
2,890

Shechem

Jabbok

(Zarqā)

Kanah

Farah

Jordan

Jebel Yusha
3,652

Joppa

Shiloh

Tell Azur
3,333

Bethel

Rabbah
(Amman)

A M M O N

Aijalon

Jericho

Plains of
Moab

Sorek

Jerusalem

Mt. of Olives
2,670

Mt. Nebo
2,631

Elah

Bethlehem

Wilderness of Judea

Dead

D e s e r t

Gaza

J U D E A

3,346

(Salt)

Shephelah

Hebron

Sea
-1,296

Arnon (W. al Maujib)

Gerar

M O A B

Besor

Raphia

Beer-sheba

Kir-hareseth

I D U M E A

Brook of Egypt

Zered (W. al Hasa)

31°N

(W. al 'Arish)

N e g e b

Wilderness of
Zin

Arabah

E D O M

Jebel Helal
2,926

34°E

Kadesh-barnea

Local grid coordinate system of 50 kilometer squares.

36°E

| 1 | U | 50 | V | 100 | W | 150 | X | 200 | Y | 250 | Z | 1 |

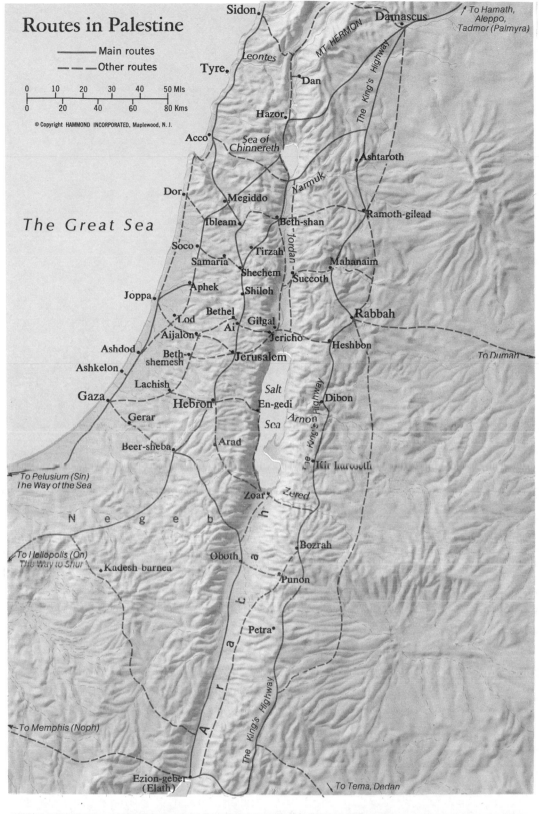

Routes in Palestine

—— Main routes
- - - Other routes

0 10 20 30 40 50 Mls
0   20   40   60   80 Kms

© Copyright HAMMOND INCORPORATED, Maplewood, N. J.

The Plain of Esdraelon looking north toward Mount Tabor.

Goats graze in the forbidding central Samaria hills, where the invading Hebrews found a home for their flocks in Biblical times.

Today children frolic in the cool waters beneath the waterfalls of En-gedi, celebrated in the Song of Songs.

The placid Dead Sea looking eastward toward the hills of Transjordan. Wind erosion at this lowest spot on earth produces an eerie, lunar landscape along the western shore.

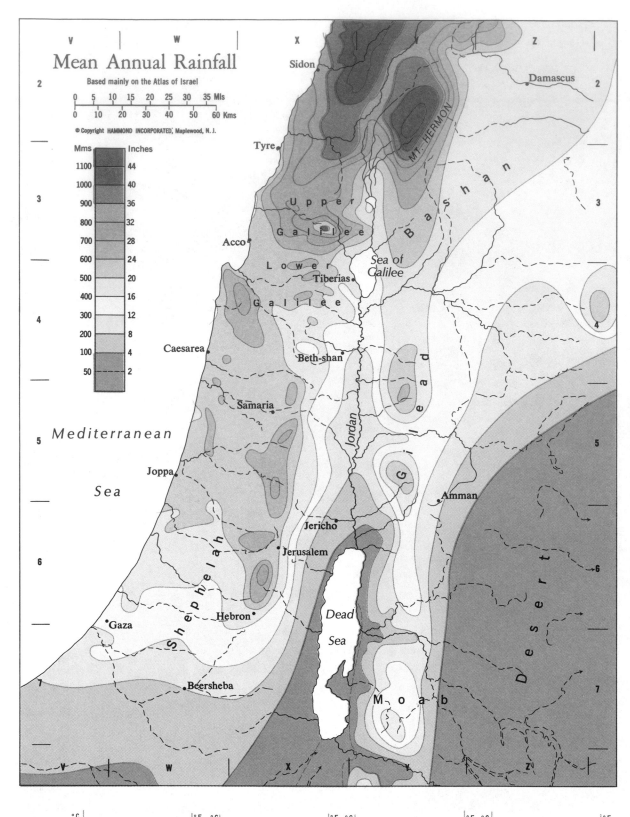

Mean Annual Rainfall

Based mainly on the Atlas of Israel

© Copyright HAMMOND INCORPORATED, Maplewood, N.J.

Mms	Inches
1100	44
1000	40
900	36
800	32
700	28
600	24
500	20
400	16
300	12
200	8
100	4
50	2

Temperature, rainfall,
and relative humidity
for selected stations

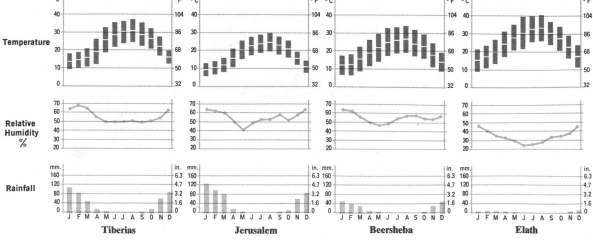

Tiberias   Jerusalem   Beersheba   Elath

© Copyright HAMMOND INC., Maplewood, N.J.

Sources: World Climatic Data, 1972; Statistical Abstract of Israel, 1969

Mean Temperature January

°Cent.	°Fahr.
16	60.8
14	57.2
12	53.6
10	50.0
8	46.4
6	42.8

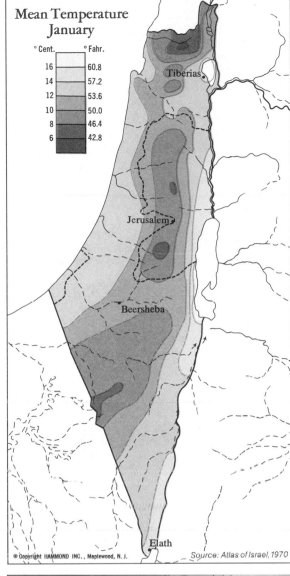

Tiberias

Jerusalem

Beersheba

Elath

© Copyright HAMMOND INC., Maplewood, N.J.   *Source: Atlas of Israel, 1970*

Mean Temperature August

°Cent.	°Fahr.
34	93.2
32	89.6
30	86.0
28	82.4
26	78.8
24	75.2
22	71.6

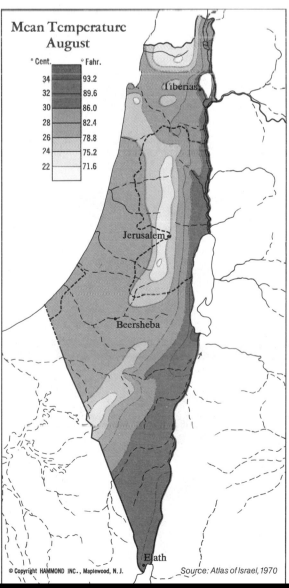

Tiberias

Jerusalem

Beersheba

Elath

© Copyright HAMMOND INC., Maplewood, N.J.   *Source: Atlas of Israel, 1970*

Economy of Palestine

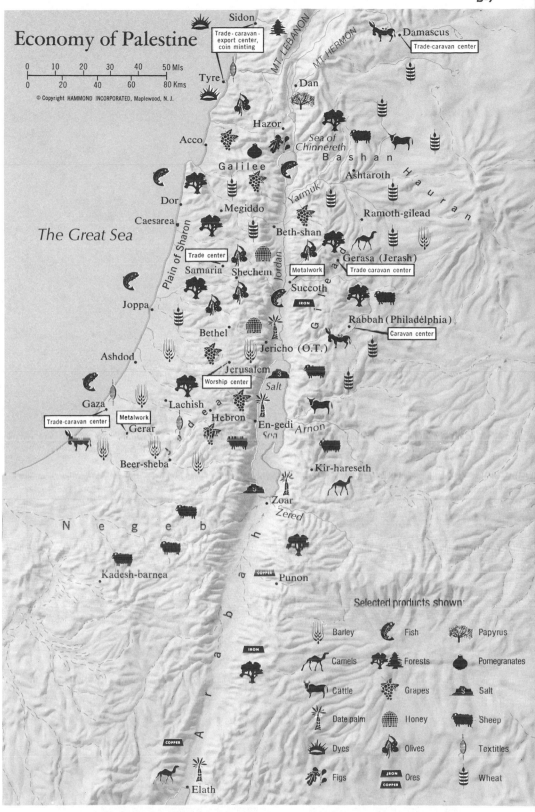

0 10 20 30 40 50 Mls
0   20   40   60 80 Kms
© Copyright HAMMOND INCORPORATED, Maplewood, N.J.

Sidon — Trade-caravan-export center, coin minting

MT. LEBANON   MT. HERMON

Damascus — Trade-caravan center

Tyre

Dan

Hazor

Acco

Sea of Chinnereth

Bashan

Galilee

Ashtaroth

Dor

Megiddo

Yarmuk

Ramoth-gilead

Caesarea

Beth-shan

The Great Sea

Plain of Sharon

Samaria

Shechem

Gerasa (Jerash) — Trade caravan center

Trade center

Metalwork

Jordan

Succoth — IRON

Joppa

Rabbah (Philadelphia) — Caravan center

Bethel

Jericho (O.T.)

Ashdod

Jerusalem — Worship center

Salt

Gaza — Trade-caravan center

Lachish

En-gedi Salt Sea

Arnon

Metalwork

Gerar

Hebron

Beer-sheba

Kir-hareseth

Negeb

Zoar

Zered

Kadesh-barnea

COPPER   Punon

IRON

COPPER

Arabah

Elath

Selected products shown:

Barley		Fish		Papyrus	
Camels		Forests		Pomegranates	
Cattle		Grapes		Salt	
Date palm		Honey		Sheep	
Dyes		Olives		Textiles	
Figs		Ores (IRON COPPER)		Wheat	

Grapes being weighed in a manner reminiscent of a period when both kings and prophets in Israel were concerned with honest measure.

A cluster of dates suggests the richness and plenty of well-watered date palm plantations such as those at Jericho.

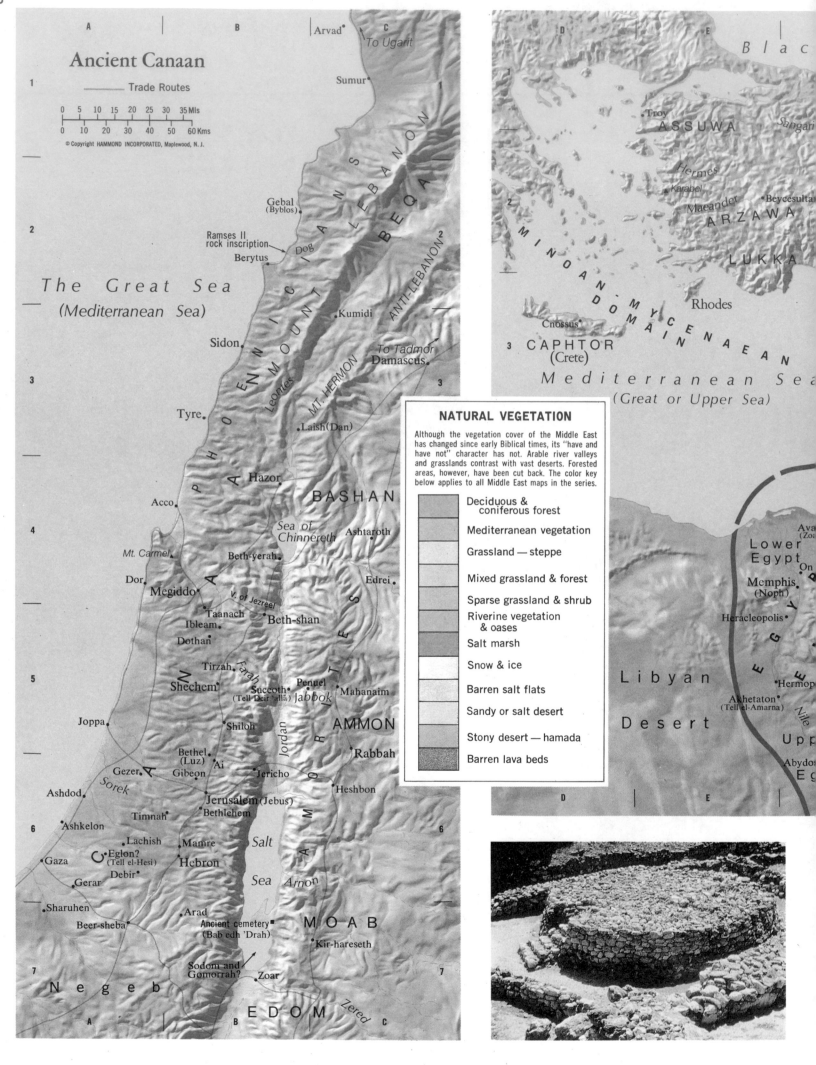

Ancient Canaan

—— Trade Routes

0 5 10 15 20 25 30 35 Mls
0 10 20 30 40 50 60 Kms

© Copyright HAMMOND INCORPORATED, Maplewood, N.J.

The Great Sea
(Mediterranean Sea)

Arvad
To Ugarit

Sumur

Gebal
(Byblos)

Ramses II
rock inscription
Berytus

Dog

Kumidi

Sidon

To Tadmor
Damascus

Tyre

Leontes

MT. HERMON

Laish (Dan)

Acco

Hazor

BASHAN

Mt. Carmel

Beth-yerah

Sea of
Chinnereth

Ashtaroth

Dor

Megiddo

V. of Jezreel

Edrei

Taanach

Beth-shan

Ibleam

Dothan

Tirzah

Farah

Shechem

Succoth
(Tell Deir 'alla)

Penuel

Jabbok

Mahanaim

Joppa

Shiloh

Jordan

AMMON

Bethel
(Luz)

Ai

Gibeon

Jericho

Rabbah

Gezer

Sorek

Heshbon

Ashdod

Jerusalem (Jebus)

Bethlehem

Timnah

Salt

Ashkelon

Lachish

Mamre

Gaza

Eglon?
(Tell el-Hesi)

Hebron

Sea

Arnon

Debir

Gerar

Sharuhen

Arad

MOAB

Beer-sheba

Ancient cemetery
(Bab edh 'Drah)

Kir-hareseth

Sodom and
Gomorrah?

Zoar

Negeb

EDOM

Zered

PHOENICIAN MOUNTAINS

LEBANON

BEQA

ANTI-LEBANON

AMORITES

Right portion

Black

ASSUWA

Troy

Sangari

Hermes

Karabel

Maeander

Beycesulta

ARZAWA

LUKKA

MINOAN-MYCENAEAN DOMAIN

Rhodes

Cnossus

CAPHTOR
(Crete)

Mediterranean Sea
(Great or Upper Sea)

Lower
Egypt

Ava
(Zoa

On

Memphis
(Noph)

Heracleopolis

Libyan

Desert

Hermop

Akhetaton
(Tell el-Amarna)

Upp

Abydos

Eg

Natural Vegetation legend

NATURAL VEGETATION

Although the vegetation cover of the Middle East has changed since early Biblical times, its "have and have not" character has not. Arable river valleys and grasslands contrast with vast deserts. Forested areas, however, have been cut back. The color key below applies to all Middle East maps in the series.

- Deciduous & coniferous forest
- Mediterranean vegetation
- Grassland — steppe
- Mixed grassland & forest
- Sparse grassland & shrub
- Riverine vegetation & oases
- Salt marsh
- Snow & ice
- Barren salt flats
- Sandy or salt desert
- Stony desert — hamada
- Barren lava beds

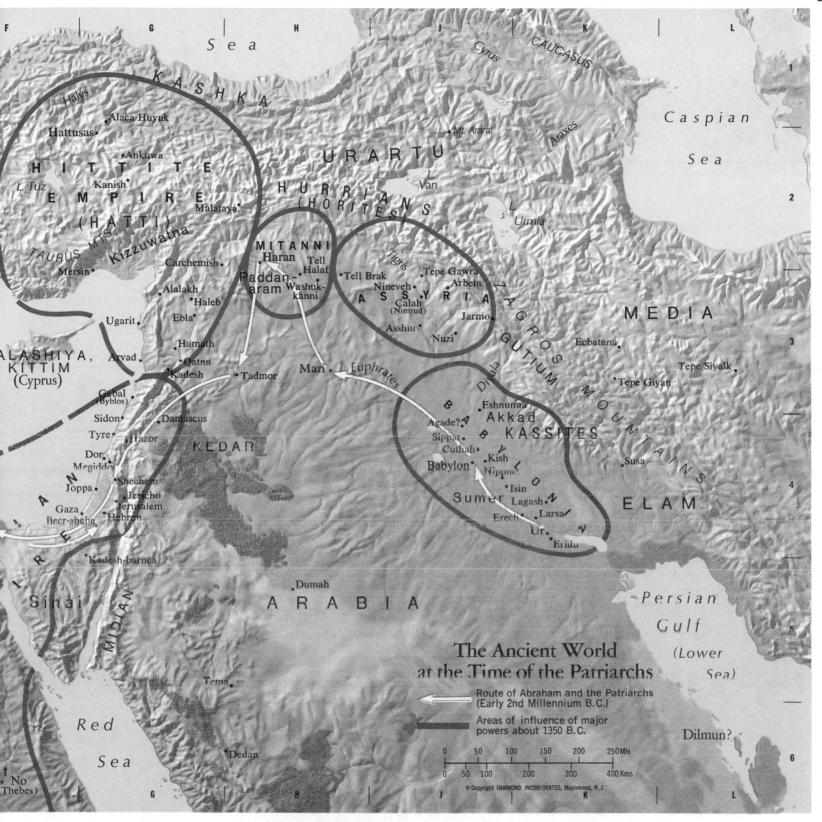

The Ancient World
at the Time of the Patriarchs

⇦ Route of Abraham and the Patriarchs
(Early 2nd Millennium B.C.)

▬ Areas of influence of major
powers about 1350 B.C.

0	50	100	150	200	250 Mls
0	50 100	200	300	400 Kms	

© Copyright HAMMOND INCORPORATED, Maplewood, N.J.

Map labels:

Sea · KASHKA · CAUCASUS · Cyrus · Caspian Sea · Halys · Alaca Huyuk · Hattusas · Ankuwa · Mt. Ararat · URARTU · Araxes · HITTITE · L. Tuz · Kanish · EMPIRE · (HATTI) · Malataya · HURRIANS (HORITES) · L. Van · L. Urmia · TAURUS MTS · Kizzuwatna · MITANNI · Haran · Tell Halaf · MEDIA · Mersin · Carchemish · Paddan-aram · Washuk-kanni · Tigris · Tepe Gawra · Arbela · Alalakh · Tell Brak · Nineveh · ASSYRIA · ZAGROS · Haleb · Calah (Nimrud) · Ebla · Asshur · Nuzi · Jarmo · Ebla · Ecbatana · ALASHIYA, KITTIM (Cyprus) · Ugarit · Arvad · Qatna · Kadesh · Tadmor · Mari · Euphrates · GUTIUM · Tepe Siyalk · Hamath · Tepe Giyan · MOUNTAINS · Gebal (Byblos) · Diyala · Eshnunna · Agade? · Akkad · KASSITES · Sidon · Damascus · Sippar · Tyre · Hazor · KEDAR · Cuthah · Kish · Susa · Dor · Megiddo · Babylon · Nippur · BABYLONIA · ELAM · Joppa · Shechem · Isin · Gaza · Jericho · Jerusalem · Sumer · Lagash · Beer-sheba · Hebron · Erech · Larsa · Kadesh-barnea · Ur · Eridu · Sinai · MIDIAN · Dumah · ARABIA · Persian Gulf (Lower Sea) · Tema · Red Sea · Dedan · Dilmun? · No (Thebes)

In the royal tombs at Ur was
found this magnificent sounding
box of a lyre. The bull's head is
of gold, silver and lapis lazuli.
Below the head are panels of
shell inlay.

The Canaanite altar for burnt
offerings at Megiddo. This
splendid "high place" was
built in the Early Bronze Age
and continued in use as late as
the 19th century B.C., the time
of the Hebrew Patriarchs.

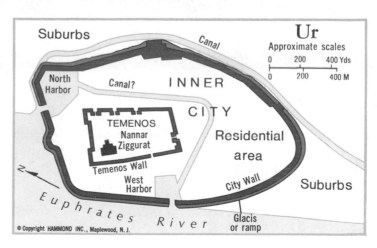

Ur
Approximate scales

0	200	400 Yds
0	200	400 M

Suburbs · Canal · North Harbor · Canal? · INNER · CITY · Residential area · TEMENOS · Nannar · Ziggurat · Temenos Wall · West Harbor · City Wall · Suburbs · N · Euphrates River · Glacis or ramp

© Copyright HAMMOND INC., Maplewood, N.J.

In a timeless scene the pyramids dominate the sandy Egyptian horizon beyond the fertile fields of the Nile River plain.

A wall painting from the reign of Thutmoses III (15th century B.C.) shows the various stages of brickmaking.

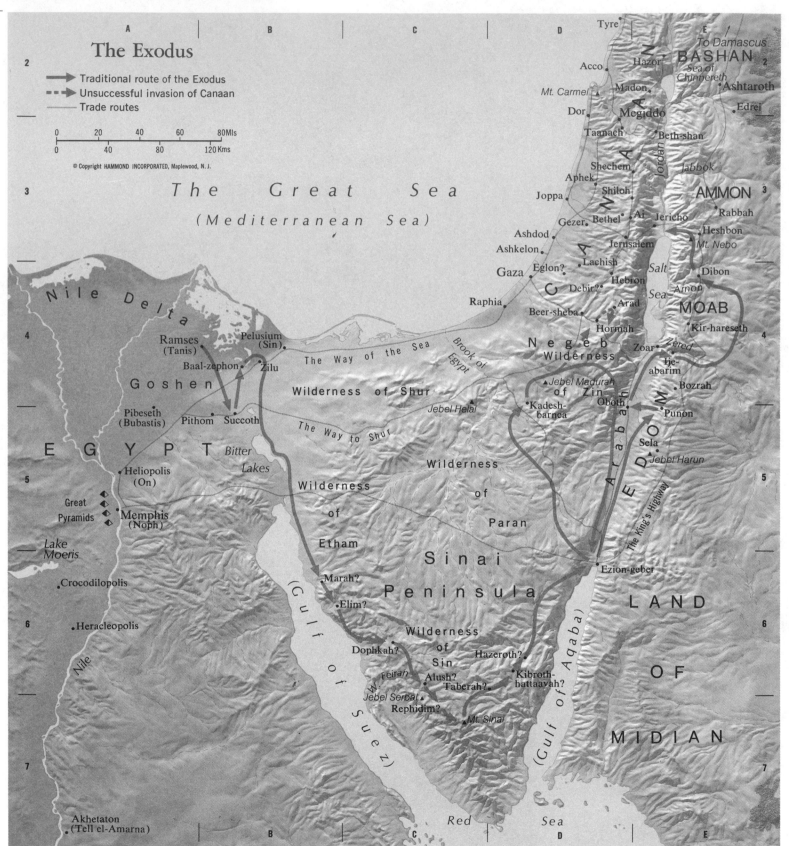

Mount Tabor, where the forces of Deborah gathered to give battle to the army of Sisera (Judges 4:6f.). A torrent turned the Esdraelon Plain (in the foreground) into a quagmire, rendering Sisera's Canaanite chariots ineffective.

A *shofar*, a type of trumpet used extensively in ancient Israel for special religious purposes in both war and peace.

Early Israelite Settlement in Canaan

Area settled by Israelites

JUDAH — Twelve Israelite tribes

Gezer — Unconquered Canaanite city (according to Judges 1)

© Copyright HAMMOND INCORPORATED, Maplewood, N. J.

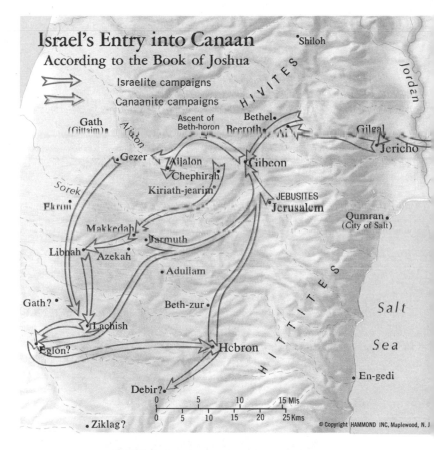

Israel's Entry into Canaan
According to the Book of Joshua

Israelite campaigns

Canaanite campaigns

© Copyright HAMMOND INC, Maplewood, N. J.

The fortress-temple of Baal-berith, probably the scene of Joshua's covenant (Joshua 24:1-28), was built at Shechem around 1650 B.C. and with modifications continued in use throughout the Period of the Judges.

Battle of Gilboa

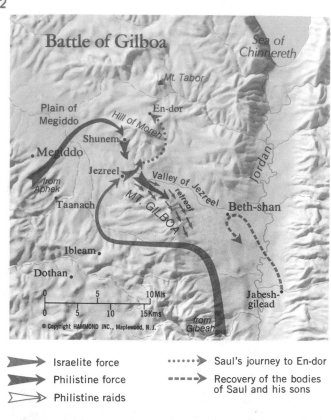

Sea of Chinnereth

Plain of Megiddo
Mt. Tabor
En-dor
Hill of Moreh
Shunem
Megiddo
Jezreel
from Aphek
Valley of Jezreel
retreat
Taanach
MT. GILBOA
Beth-shan
Ibleam
retreat
Jordan
Dothan
Jabesh-gilead
from Gibeah

0 5 10Mls
0 5 10 15Kms
© Copyright HAMMOND INC., Maplewood, N.J.

→ Israelite force
→ Philistine force
▷ Philistine raids
····▷ Saul's journey to En-dor
---▷ Recovery of the bodies of Saul and his sons

Battle of Michmash

Ophrah
Bethel
Lower Beth-horon
Upper Beth-horon
Michmash
Gilgal
Aijalon
retreat
Geba
Gibeon
to Geba
Kiriath-jearim
Gibeah
to Michmash
Jerusalem
Beth-shemesh
Wilderness of Judah
Bethlehem
Salt Sea

0 5 10 15Mls
0 5 10 15 20 25Kms
© Copyright HAMMOND INC., Maplewood, N.J.

The Kingdom of Saul

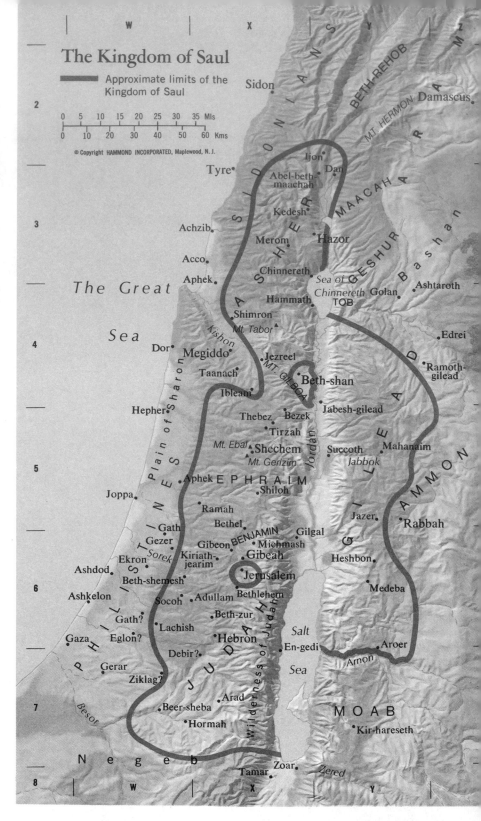

━━━ Approximate limits of the Kingdom of Saul

0 5 10 15 20 25 30 35 Mls
0 10 20 30 40 50 60 Kms
© Copyright HAMMOND INCORPORATED, Maplewood, N.J.

W   X   Y

Sidon
BETH-REHOB
MT. HERMON
Damascus
Tyre
Ijon
Dan
Abel-beth-maachah
MAACAH
ASHER
GESHUR
Kedesh
Achzib
Merom
Hazor
Bashan
Acco
Chinnereth
Sea of Chinnereth
Ashtaroth
Aphek
Hammath
TOB
Golan
The Great Sea
Shimron
Mt. Tabor
Edrei
Kishon
Dor
Megiddo
Jezreel
MT. GILBOA
Ramoth-gilead
Taanach
Beth-shan
GILEAD
Ibleam
Jabesh-gilead
Hepher
Thebez
Bezek
Plain of Sharon
Mt. Ebal
Tirzah
Shechem
Succoth
Mahanaim
Mt. Gerizim
Jabbok
Aphek
EPHRAIM
Joppa
Shiloh
AMMON
Ramah
Jazer
Rabbah
Gath
Bethel
Gezer
Gibeon
Gilgal
BENJAMIN
Ekron
Sorek
Kiriath-jearim
Michmash
Heshbon
Ashdod
Gibeah
Beth-shemesh
Jerusalem
Ashkelon
Socoh
Adullam
Bethlehem
Medeba
Gath?
Beth-zur
PHILISTIA
Lachish
Gaza
Eglon?
Debir?
JUDAH
Hebron
En-gedi
Salt Sea
Aroer
Gerar
Ziklag?
Wilderness of Judah
Arnon
Besor
Arad
Negeb
Beer-sheba
MOAB
Hormah
Kir-hareseth
Tamar
Zoar
Zered
W   X   Y

Central Judah and Philistia

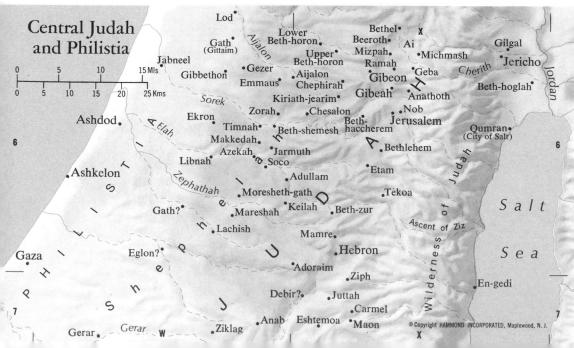

0 5 10 15Mls
0 5 10 15 20 25 Kms

Lod
Bethel
Gath (Gittaim)
Lower Beth-horon
Beeroth
Ai
Gilgal
Jabneel
Aijalon
Upper Beth-horon
Mizpah
Michmash
Jericho
Gezer
Ramah
Geba
Cherith
Gibbethon
Aijalon
Chephirah
Gibeon
Beth-hoglah
Emmaus
Kiriath-jearim
Anathoth
Sorek
Gibeah
Jordan
Ashdod
Ekron
Zorah
Chesalon
Nob
Timnah
Beth-haccherem
Jerusalem
Makkedah
Beth-shemesh
Qumran (City of Salt)
Elah
Azekah
Jarmuth
Bethlehem
Libnah
Soco
Ashkelon
Zephathah
Adullam
Etam
Salt Sea
Moresheth-gath
Tekoa
Gath?
Keilah
Beth-zur
Gaza
Mareshah
Mamre
Lachish
Wilderness of Judah
Eglon?
Hebron
Ascent of Ziz
Adoraim
Ziph
Debir?
Juttah
Wilderness of Zin
En-gedi
Carmel
Gerar
Anab
Eshtemoa
Maon
Gerar
Ziklag
© Copyright HAMMOND INCORPORATED, Maplewood, N.J.

At Gibeah the remains of Saul's fortress-palace (background) are surrounded by later construction (foreground). The rude simplicity of Saul's capital contrasted sharply with Solomon's magnificent buildings constructed four miles away in Jerusalem only a few years later.

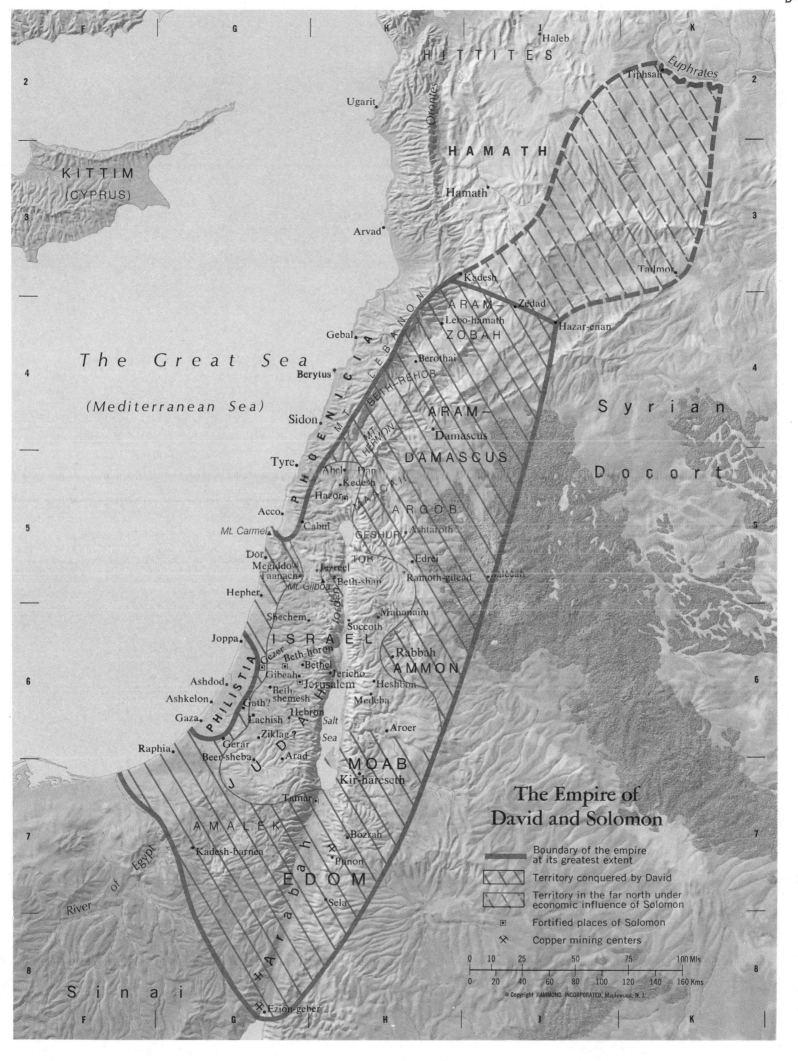

KITTIM
(CYPRUS)

The Great Sea

(Mediterranean Sea)

HITTITES

Haleb

Euphrates

Ugarit

Orontes

HAMATH

Hamath

Arvad

Tiphsah

Kadesh

Zedad

ARAM –

Lebo-hamath

Hazar-enan

Gebal

ZOBAH

Berothai

Berytus

BETH-REHOB

ARAM –

S y r i a n

Sidon

MT. HERMON

DAMASCUS

Damascus

D e s e r t

Tyre

Abel

Dan

Kedesh

MAACAH

Hazor

ARGOB

Acco

Cabul

GESHUR

Ashtaroth

Mt. Carmel

Dor

TOB

Edrei

Megiddo

Jezreel

Taanach

Mt. Gilboa

Beth-shan

Ramoth-gilead

Halecah

Hepher

Mahanaim

Shechem

Succoth

Joppa

ISRAEL

Rabbah

Gezer

Beth-horon

AMMON

PHILISTIA

Gibeah

Bethel

Jericho

Heshbon

Ashdod

Beth-shemesh

Jerusalem

Medeba

Ashkelon

Gath?

Hebron

Gaza

Lachish

Salt

Aroer

Ziklag?

Sea

Raphia

Gerar

JUDAH

Arad

Beer-sheba

Tamar

MOAB

Kir-hareseth

AMALEK

Bozrah

Kadesh-barnea

Punon

River of Egypt

EDOM

Arabah

Sela

S i n a i

Ezion-geber

The Empire of
David and Solomon

— Boundary of the empire
at its greatest extent

Territory conquered by David

Territory in the far north under
economic influence of Solomon

▣ Fortified places of Solomon

⚒ Copper mining centers

0 10 25   50   75   100 Mls

0 20 40 60 80 100 120 140 160 Kms

® Copyright HAMMOND INCORPORATED, Maplewood, N. J.

The Israelite gate at Gezer is one of the finest Solomonic structures yet found. Its design of two outer towers and six flanking guardrooms is virtually identical to Solomon's fortification gates at Megiddo and Hazor.

Solomonic Gate at Gezer

0 5 10 Yds
0 5 10 M

A proto-Ionic capital of the type that graced the gates of the royal cities and palaces of Israel and Judah: Samaria, Megiddo, Hazor, Ramat Rahel and most likely Jerusalem and Gezer.

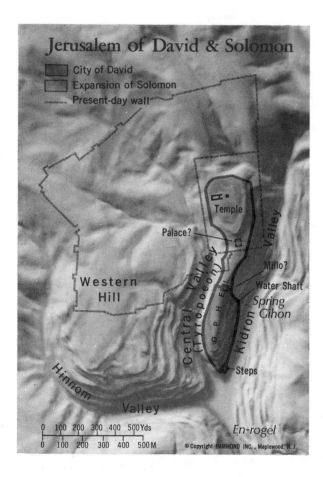

Jerusalem of David & Solomon

- City of David
- Expansion of Solomon
- Present-day wall

Temple
Palace?
Western Hill
Central Valley (Tyropoeon)
OPHEL
Millo?
Water Shaft
Spring Gihon
Kidron Valley
Steps
Hinnom Valley
En-rogel

0 100 200 300 400 500 Yds
0 100 200 300 400 500 M
© Copyright HAMMOND INC., Maplewood, N.J.

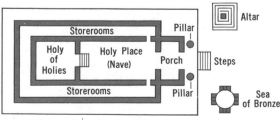

Storerooms
Holy of Holies
Holy Place (Nave)
Porch
Pillar
Storerooms
Pillar
Altar
Steps
Sea of Bronze

Temple of Solomon

0 10 20 30 Cubits
0 5 10 15 M

Solomon's Twelve Districts

Boundary of tax districts
Gezer Royal City of Solomon
▣ Places fortified by Solomon

0 5 10 15 20 25 30 35 Mls
0 10 20 30 40 50 60 Kms
© Copyright HAMMOND INCORPORATED, Maplewood, N.J.

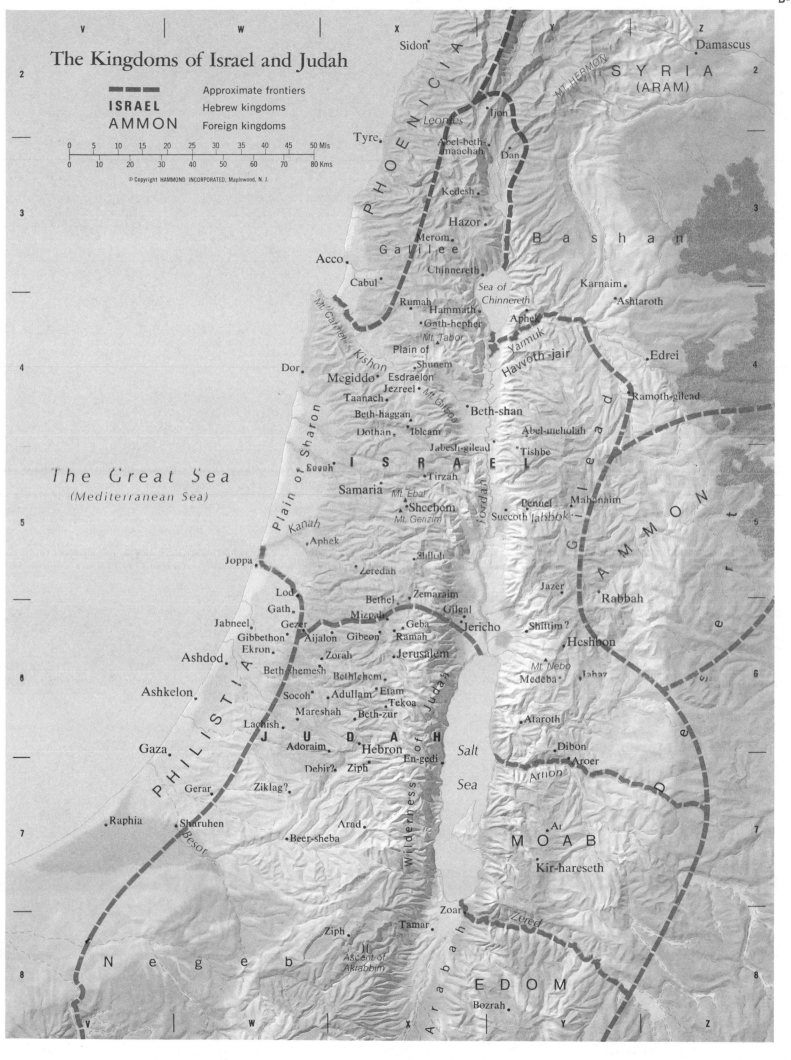

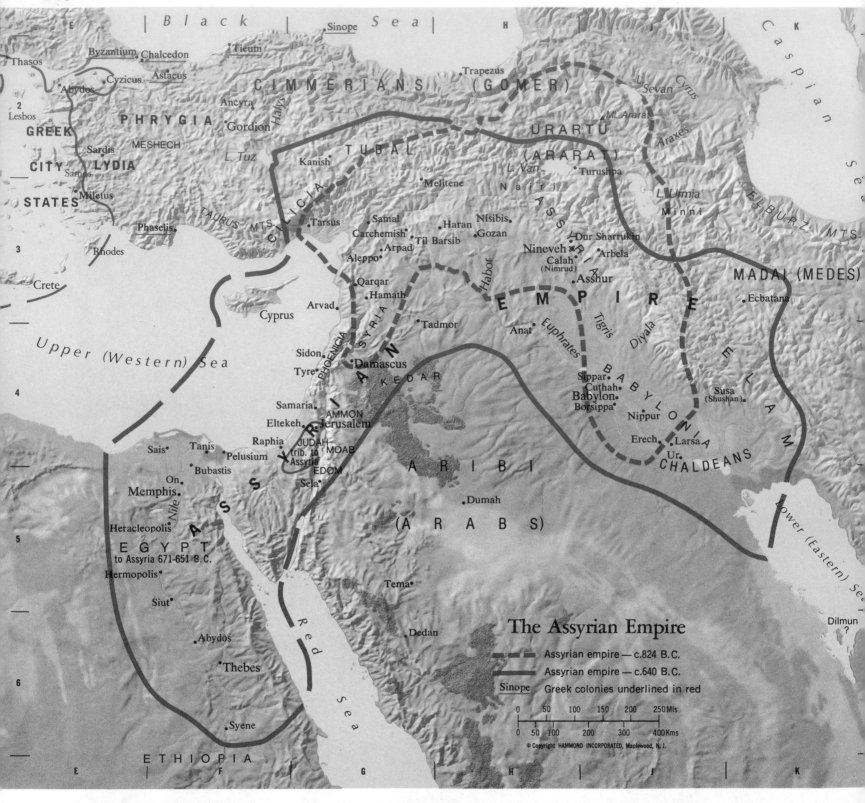

Black Sea

Sinope

Thasos
Byzantium Chalcedon
Cyzicus Astacus Tieum
Abydos
Lesbos
GREEK Sardis
CITY Samos **LYDIA**
STATES Miletus
Phaselis
Rhodes
Crete

Trapezus

CIMMERIANS **(GOMER)**

PHRYGIA Gordion
MESHECH Ancyra
L. Tuz
Kanish
TUBAL
Melitene

URARTU
(ARARAT) Mt. Ararat
L. Van Turushpa
N a i r i
L. Urmia
Minni
L. Sevan

Cyrus
Araxes

ELBURZ MTS.

Caspian Sea

TAURUS MTS.
CILICIA Tarsus
Samal Carchemish
Aleppo Arpad Til Barsib
Haran
Nisibis
Gozan

Dur Sharrukin
Nineveh
Calah Arbela
(Nimrud)
Asshur

MADAI (MEDES)
Ecbatana

Qarqar
Hamath
Arvad
Cyprus
Tadmor

E M P I R E
Habor

Anat
Euphrates
Tigris
Diyala

E L A M

Sippar
Cuthah **BABYLONIA**
Babylon
Borsippa
Nippur

Susa
(Shushan)

Upper (Western) Sea

Sidon
Tyre PHOENICIA
Damascus
A KEDAR
Samaria
Eltekeh **AMMON**
Jerusalem
Raphia **JUDAH**
trib. to **MOAB**
Assyria **EDOM**
Sela

S Y R I A

Erech Larsa
Ur
CHALDEANS

Sais
Tanis
Pelusium
Bubastis
On
Memphis

A S S Y R I A

A R I B I
Dumah

(A R A B S)

Lower (Eastern) Sea

Heracleopolis
E G Y P T
to Assyria 671-651 B.C.
Hermopolis
Siut

Tema

Dilmun?

Abydos
Thebes

Red Sea

Dedan

Syene

E T H I O P I A

The Assyrian Empire

– – – Assyrian empire — c.824 B.C.
——— Assyrian empire — c.640 B.C.
Sinope Greek colonies underlined in red

0 50 100 150 200 250 Mls
0 50 100 200 300 400 Kms

© Copyright HAMMOND INCORPORATED, Maplewood, N.J.

Tiglath-pileser III extended the
Assyrian Empire in the 8th
century B.C. and caused political
chaos in Israel.

The only contemporary picture of a Hebrew
monarch occurs on the Black Obelisk, an
Assyrian monument from Nimrud. It shows
Jehu on his knees before Shalmaneser III.

Assyrian wall relief from the throne room of
Sennacherib shows Hebrews fleeing the doomed
city of Lachish in southwest Judah when it was
under Assyrian siege in 701 B.C.

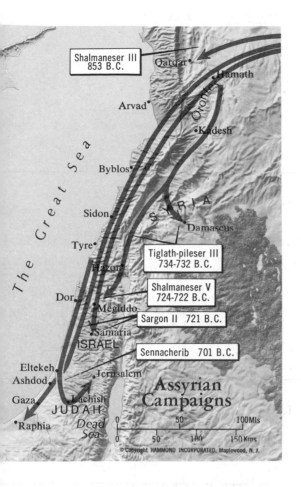

Assyrian Campaigns

Shalmaneser III 853 B.C.

Tiglath-pileser III 734-732 B.C.

Shalmaneser V 724-722 B.C.

Sargon II 721 B.C.

Sennacherib 701 B.C.

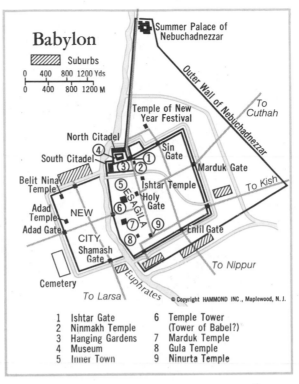

Babylon

Suburbs

0	400	800	1200 Yds
0	400	800	1200 M

Summer Palace of Nebuchadnezzar

Temple of New Year Festival

North Citadel

South Citadel

Belit Nina Temple

Adad Temple

Adad Gate

NEW CITY

Shamash Gate

Cemetery

Sin Gate

Marduk Gate

Ishtar Temple

Holy Gate

ESAGILA

Enlil Gate

To Cuthah

To Kish

To Nippur

To Larsa

Euphrates

Outer Wall of Nebuchadnezzar

© Copyright HAMMOND INC., Maplewood, N.J.

1 Ishtar Gate
2 Ninmakh Temple
3 Hanging Gardens
4 Museum
5 Inner Town
6 Temple Tower (Tower of Babel?)
7 Marduk Temple
8 Gula Temple
9 Ninurta Temple

A reconstruction of the Ishtar Gate at Babylon, with the famous "hanging gardens" in the right background. The king entering the gate is Nebuchadnezzar II (605-562 B.C.), who destroyed Jerusalem.

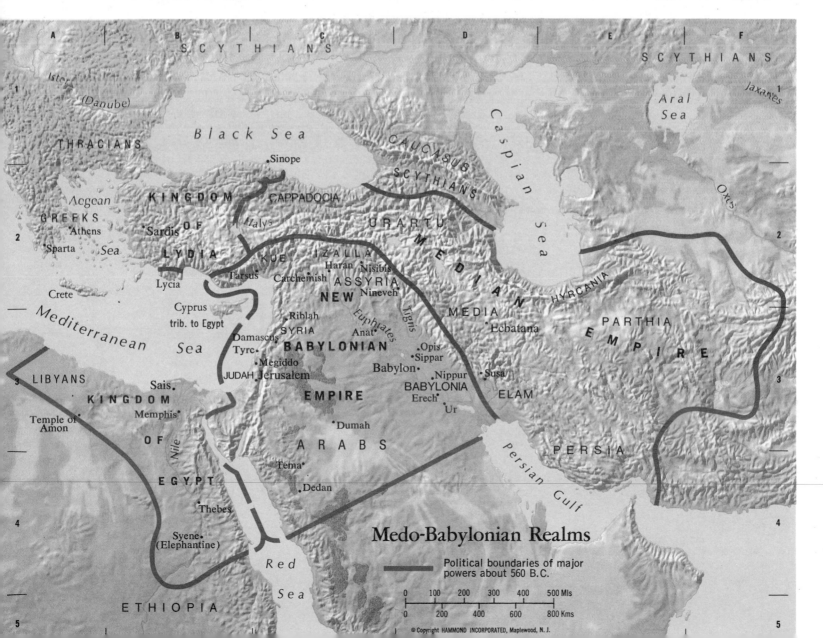

Medo-Babylonian Realms

Political boundaries of major powers about 560 B.C.

0	100	200	300	400	500 Mls
0	200	400	600	800 Kms	

© Copyright HAMMOND INCORPORATED, Maplewood, N.J.

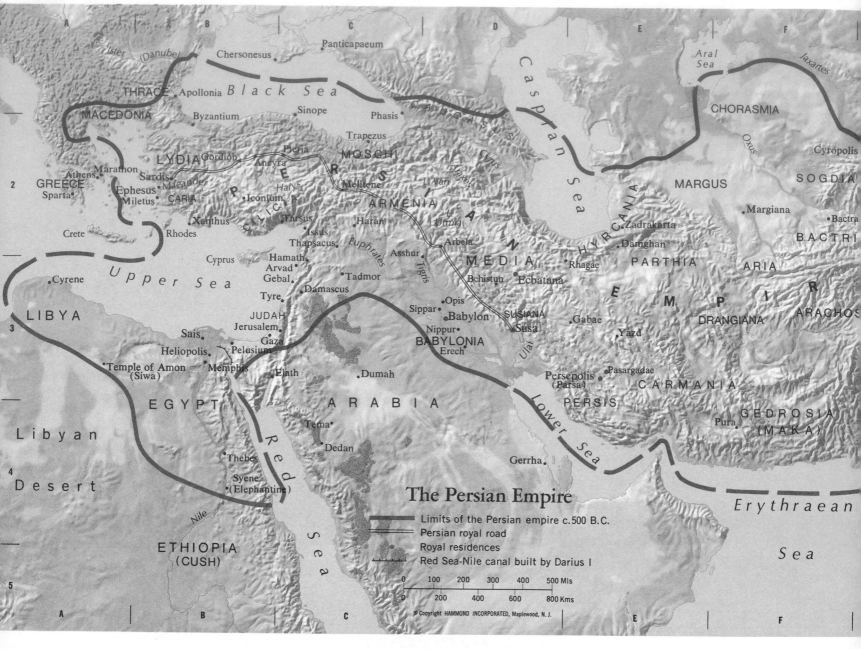

The Persian Empire

Limits of the Persian empire c. 500 B.C.
Persian royal road
Royal residences
Red Sea-Nile canal built by Darius I

| 0 | 100 | 200 | 300 | 400 | 500 Mls |
| 0 | 200 | 400 | 600 | 800 Kms |

© Copyright HAMMOND INCORPORATED, Maplewood, N.J.

On this clay cylinder of 538 B.C., Cyrus provides royal authorization for the rebuilding of temples "beyond the Euphrates."

Tomb of Cyrus the Great at Pasargadae, Iran. When he conquered Babylon, Cyrus allowed the Jews to return to Jerusalem and rebuild their temple.

The earliest coin used in the Holy Land is this 4th-century silver Persian piece. The obverse has a falcon with the inscription "Yahud." The reverse has a lily with no inscription.

Jerusalem After the Exile

Post-exilic city
Expansion of city
Present-day wall

Large-scale expansion of the city to the western hill is unlikely until 2nd or 3rd century B.C. although there was some building here as early as the 8th century B.C.

Tower of Hananel

Temple

Nehemiah's Wall

Spring Gihon

Central Valley

Kidron Valley

Hinnom

Pool of Siloam

Hezekiah's Aqueduct

Valley

En-rogel

| 0 | 100 | 200 | 300 | 400 | 500 Yds |
| 0 | 100 | 200 | 300 | 400 | 500 M |

© Copyright HAMMOND INC., Maplewood, N.J.

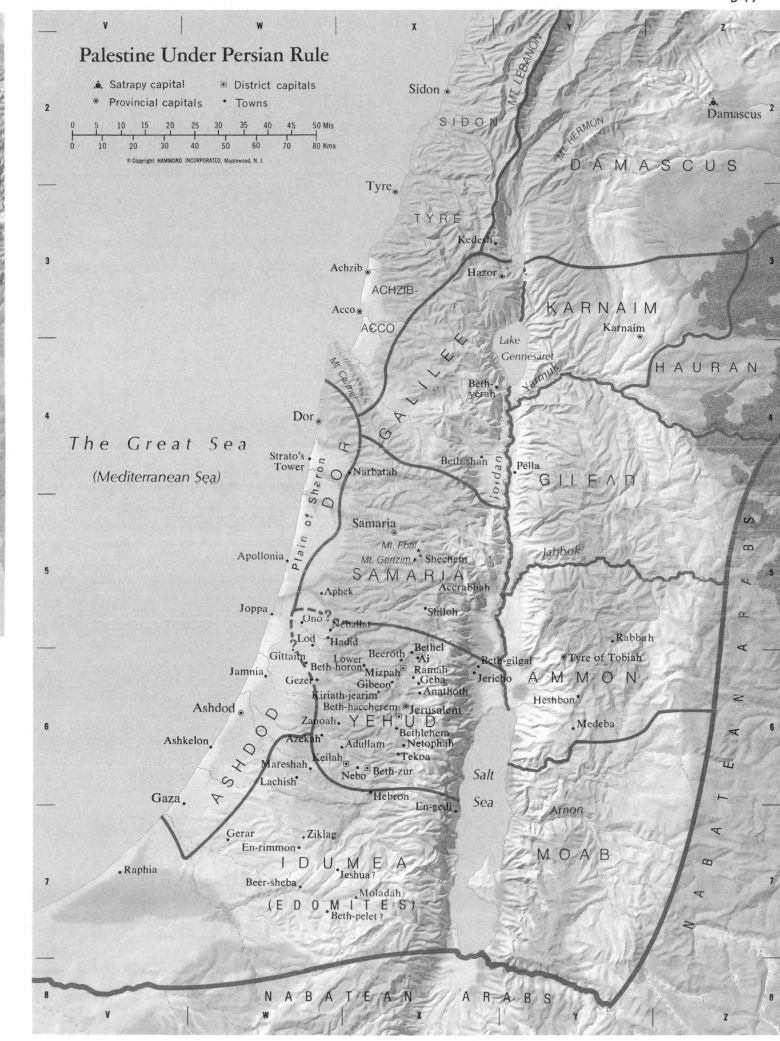

Palestine Under Persian Rule

- ⛰ Satrapy capital
- ◉ Provincial capitals
- ▣ District capitals
- • Towns

```
0   5   10   15   20   25   30   35   40   45   50 Mls
0   10    20      30    40    50     60     70    80 Kms
```

© Copyright HAMMOND INCORPORATED, Maplewood, N.J.

THIANS (AKA)

HINDU KUSH

ophen abul)

ANDARA

• Taxila

INDUSH (INDIA)

iala

Probable ancient coastline

The Great Sea

(Mediterranean Sea)

SIDON

Sidon •

TYRE

Tyre ◉

Kedesh •

Achzib ◉

ACHZIB-

Acco ◉

ACCO

Mt. Carmel

Dor ◉

Strato's Tower

Narbatah

Apollonia •

Joppa •

Ono • Neballat

Lod • Hadid •

Gittaim •

Jamnia •

Gezer •

Ashdod ◉

Ashkelon •

ASHDOD

Gaza •

Gerar • Ziklag •

En-rimmon •

IDUMEA

Raphia •

Beer-sheba •   Jeshua?

Moladah •

(E D O M I T E S)

Beth-pelet ?

Mt. Lebanon

Mt. Hermon

Damascus ⛰

D A M A S C U S

KARNAIM

Hazor ◉

Karnaim ◉

HAURAN

Lake Gennesaret

Beth-yerah

Yarmuk

Beth-shan

Pella •

Jordan

GILEAD

Jabbok

SAMARIA

Samaria ◉

Mt. Ebal

Mt. Gerizim • Shechem

Accrabbah

Aphek •

Shiloh •

Rabbah •

Bethel •

Beeroth • Ai •

Lower   Ramah •

Beth-horon Mizpah ▣   Geba •

Gibeon • Anathoth •

Kiriath-jearim •

Beth-haccherem • Jerusalem ◉

Zanoah • YEHUD

Azekah • Bethlehem •

Adullam • Netophah •

Keilah • Tekoa •

Mareshah ▣ Nebo ▣ Beth-zur ▣

Lachish •

Hebron •

En-gedi •

Beth-gilgal • Tyre of Tobiah •

Jericho •

AMMON

Heshbon •

Medeba •

Salt Sea

Arnon

MOAB

N A B A T E A N   A R A B S

N A B A T E A N   A R A B S

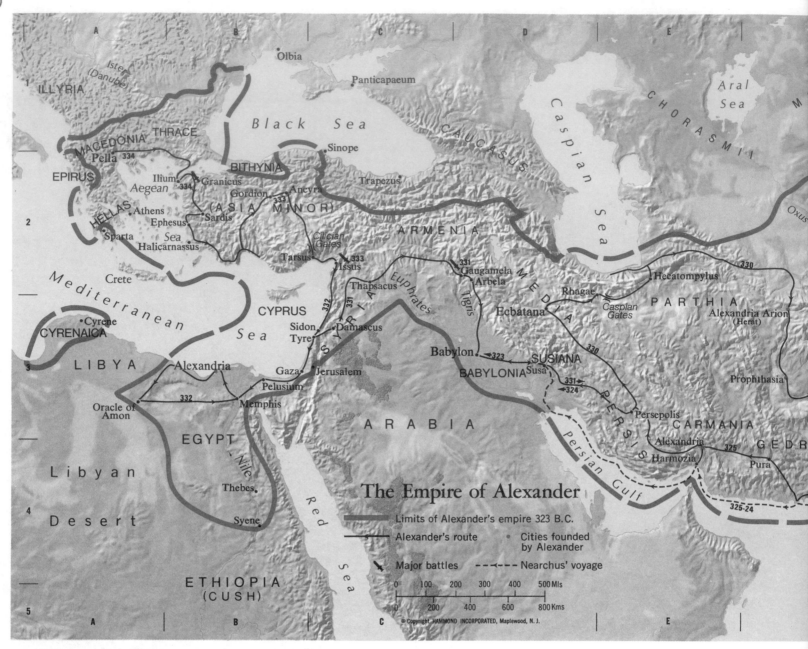

The Empire of Alexander

— Limits of Alexander's empire 323 B.C.

— Alexander's route • Cities founded by Alexander

✈ Major battles --◄-- Nearchus' voyage

0 100 200 300 400 500 Mls
0 200 400 600 800 Kms

© Copyright HAMMOND INCORPORATED, Maplewood, N.J.

Alexander the Great at the Battle of Issus, where he defeated the Persians. This Roman mosaic from Pompeii shows the determination of this brilliant soldier who established an empire at age thirty.

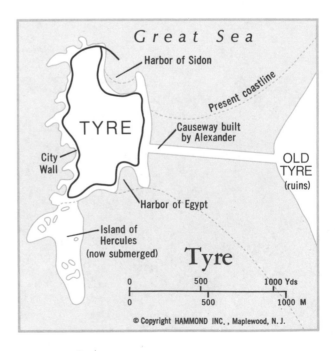

Tyre

Great Sea

Harbor of Sidon

Present coastline

TYRE

Causeway built by Alexander

City Wall

OLD TYRE (ruins)

Harbor of Egypt

Island of Hercules (now submerged)

0 500 1000 Yds
0 500 1000 M

© Copyright HAMMOND INC., Maplewood, N.J.

Silver tetradrachm of Ptolemy I struck in Egypt shows Alexander wearing an elephant head-dress. Reverse: the goddess Athena.

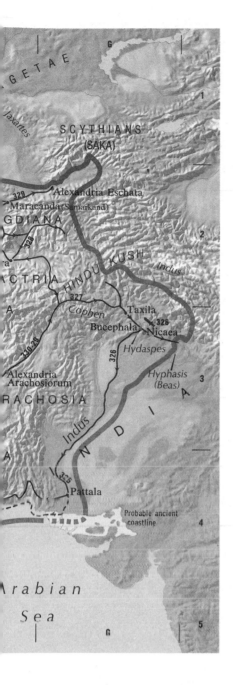

Seleucus I, "Nicator," continued Alexander's Hellenizing policies.

Ptolemy I, "Soter," turned Egypt into his personal domain.

Massive round towers such as this one were set into Israelite walls at Samaria by Alexander's military engineers. Samaria, once capital of Israel, became one of the most Hellenized cities of Palestine.

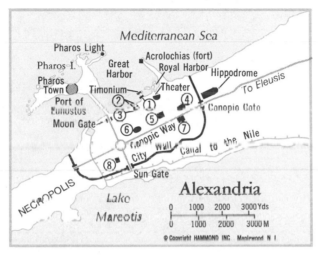

Alexandria

1 Poseidium	5 Library and Museum
2 Obelisks (later Cleopatra's Needles)	6 Amphitheater
3 Caesarium	7 Sports Grounds
4 Stadium	8 Serapeion

Terracotta statuette of a war elephant with driver and tower.

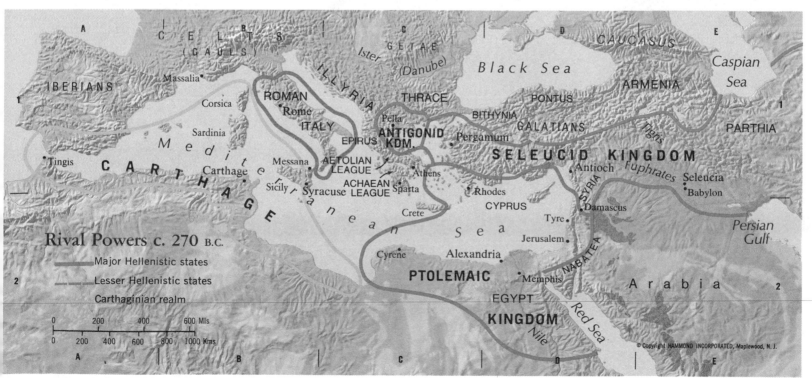

Rival Powers c. 270 B.C.

——— Major Hellenistic states

– – – Lesser Hellenistic states

——— Carthaginian realm

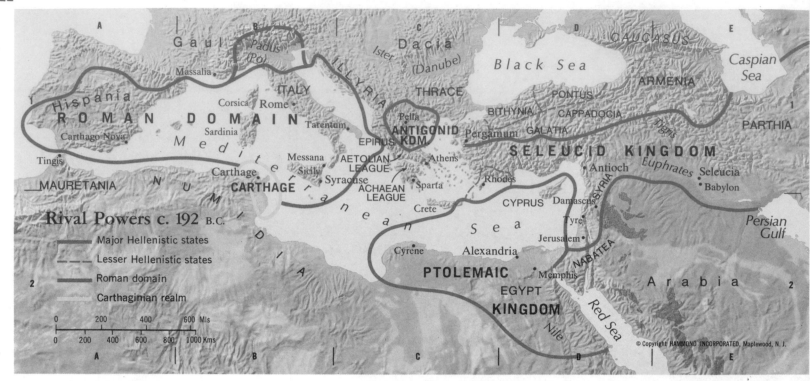

Rival Powers c. 192 B.C.

— Major Hellenistic states
--- Lesser Hellenistic states
— Roman domain
— Carthaginian realm

Antiochus III, "The Great," who took Palestine from the Ptolemies at the Battle of Panias in 197 B.C.

Naked Greek youths participating in athletic contests are pictured on this 6th-century B.C. Greek vase. Such practices introduced into Jerusalem were a cause of the Maccabean Revolt.

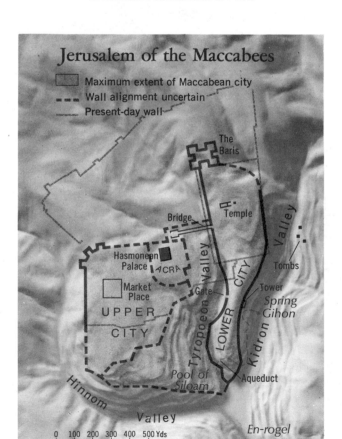

Jerusalem of the Maccabees

▨ Maximum extent of Maccabean city
--- Wall alignment uncertain
— Present-day wall

Antiochus IV, "Epiphanes," tried to Hellenize the Jews, which led to the Maccabean War in 166 B.C.

A lepton of Alexander Jannaeus (103-76 B.C.), who expanded the Jewish Hasmonean Kingdom to its greatest limits. This coin is popularly known as the "widow's mite" of the New Testament. (Mark 12:42, Luke 21:2).

A Jewish "slipper lamp" from the time of the Hasmonean Kingdom.

Antigonus II (40-37 B.C.), the last of the Hasmonean rulers, issued debased coinage, but did show the Menorah on some coins such as this perutah. He lost his throne to Herod the Great.

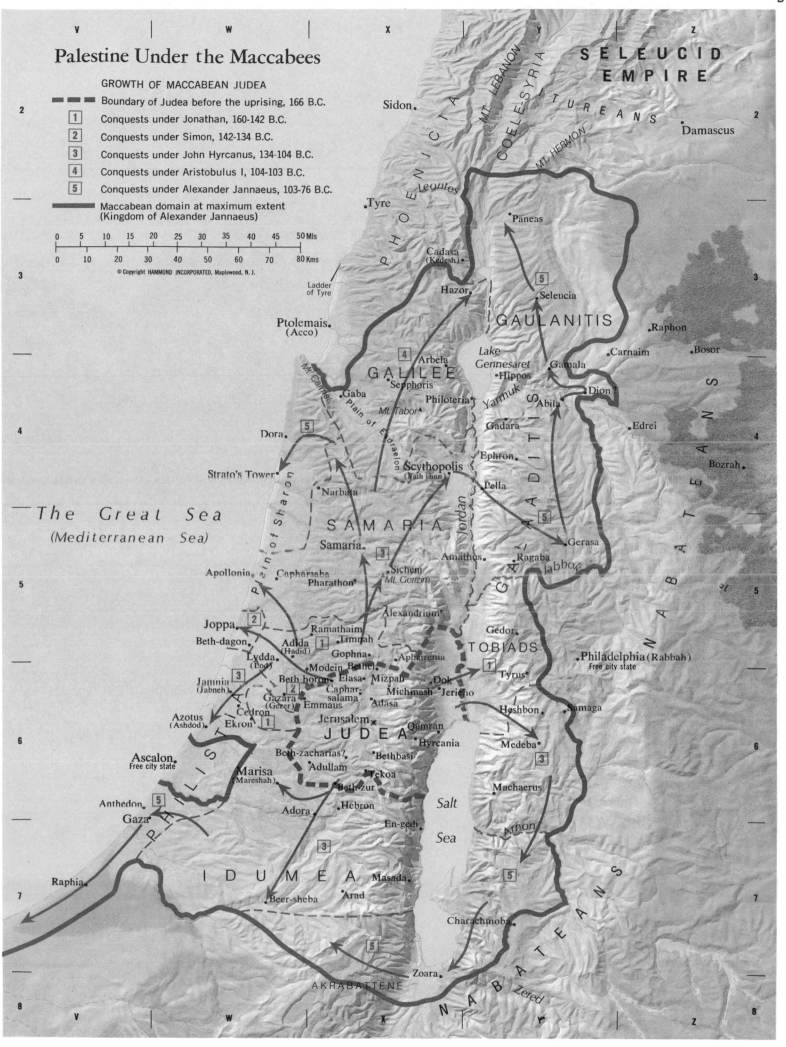

Palestine Under the Maccabees

GROWTH OF MACCABEAN JUDEA

- - - - Boundary of Judea before the uprising, 166 B.C.
1 Conquests under Jonathan, 160-142 B.C.
2 Conquests under Simon, 142-134 B.C.
3 Conquests under John Hyrcanus, 134-104 B.C.
4 Conquests under Aristobulus I, 104-103 B.C.
5 Conquests under Alexander Jannaeus, 103-76 B.C.
━━━ Maccabean domain at maximum extent
(Kingdom of Alexander Jannaeus)

0 5 10 15 20 25 30 35 40 45 50 Mls
0 10 20 30 40 50 60 70 80 Kms

© Copyright HAMMOND INCORPORATED, Maplewood, N. J.

SELEUCID EMPIRE

PHOENICIA
COELE-SYRIA
ITUREANS
MT. LEBANON
MT. HERMON
Sidon
Damascus

Tyre
Leontes
Paneas
Cadasa (Kedesh)
Hazor
Seleucia
GAULANITIS
Raphon

Ptolemais (Acco)
Ladder of Tyre
Arbela
GALILEE
Lake Gennesaret
Hippos
Gamala
Carnaim
Bosor

Mt. Carmel
Gaba
Sepphoris
Philoteria
Dion?
Abila

Dora
Mt. Tabor
Plain of Esdraelon
Yarmuk
Gadara
Edrei

Strato's Tower
Scythopolis (Beth-shan)
Ephron
Bozrah

The Great Sea
(Mediterranean Sea)
Narbata
Pella
GADARITIS

Samaria
SAMARIA
Jordan
Amathus
Gerasa
NABATEANS

Apollonia
Capharsaba
Sichem
Mt. Gerizim
Ragaba
Jabbok

Pharathon
Alexandrium
Gedor
Philadelphia (Rabbah) Free city state

Joppa
Ramathaim
Timnah
TOBIADS
Beth-dagon
Adida (Hadid)
Gophna
Aphaerema
Tyrus
Lydda (Lod)
Modein
Bethel
Dok
Jamnia (Jabneh)
Beth-horon
Elasa
Mizpah
Michmash
Jericho
Heshbon
Samaga
Gazara (Gezer)
Caphar-salama
Emmaus
Adasa
Azotus (Ashdod)
Cedron
Ekron
Jerusalem
JUDEA
Qumran
Medeba
Ascalon Free city state
Hyrcania
Beth-zacharias?
Bethbasi
Adullam
Bethbasi
Tekoa
Marisa (Mareshah)
Beth-zur
Machaerus
PHILISTIA
Anthedon
Adora
Hebron
En-gedi
Salt Sea
Gaza
Beer-sheba
Arad
Masada
Arnon
Raphia
IDUMEA
Charachmoba
AKRABATTENE
Zoara
Zered
NABATEANS

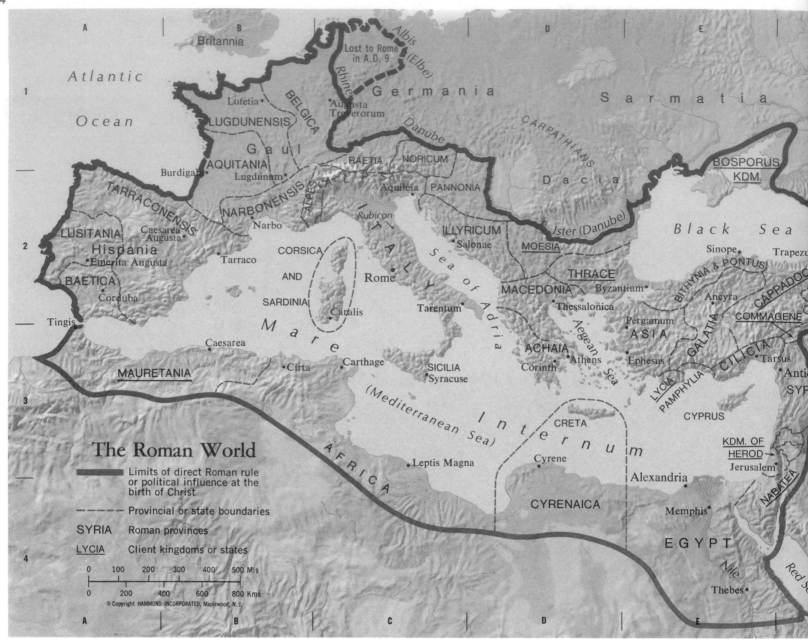

The Roman World

—— Limits of direct Roman rule or political influence at the birth of Christ

- - - - Provincial or state boundaries

SYRIA — Roman provinces

<u>LYCIA</u> — Client kingdoms or states

```
0   100   200   300   400   500 Mls
0     200     400     600     800 Kms
```
© Copyright HAMMOND INCORPORATED, Maplewood, N.J.

Britannia
Atlantic Ocean
Germania
Lost to Rome in A.D. 9
Albis (Elbe)
Rhine
Sarmatia
Lutetia
BELGICA
LUGDUNENSIS
Augusta Treverorum
Danube
CARPATHIANS
Gaul
AQUITANIA
Burdigala
Lugdunum
RAETIA
NORICUM
Aquileia
PANNONIA
ALPES
ALPS
Dacia
BOSPORUS KDM.
TARRACONENSIS
NARBONENSIS
Narbo
Rubicon
ILLYRICUM
Ister (Danube)
Black Sea
LUSITANIA
Hispania
Caesarea Augusta
CORSICA
ITALY
Salonae
MOESIA
Sinope
Trapezu
Emerita Augusta
Tarraco
AND
Rome
Sea of Adria
THRACE
BITHYNIA & PONTUS
BAETICA
SARDINIA
MACEDONIA
Byzantium
Corduba
Caralis
Tarentum
Thessalonica
Pergamum
ASIA
GALATIA
CAPPADOC
COMMAGENE
Tingis
Caesarea
Mare
SICILIA
Syracuse
ACHAIA
Corinth
Athens
Aegean Sea
Ephesus
LYCIA
PAMPHYLIA
CILICIA
Tarsus
Anti
SYR
MAURETANIA
Cirta
Carthage
Internum
CYPRUS
AFRICA
(Mediterranean Sea)
CRETA
Cyrene
KDM. OF HEROD
Alexandria
Jerusalem
NABATEA
Leptis Magna
CYRENAICA
Memphis
EGYPT
Nile
Thebes
Red S

Senate House in the Imperial Forum.

Octavian (Caesar Augustus).

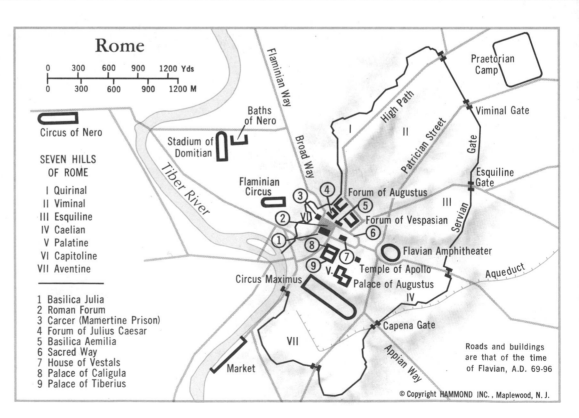

Rome

```
0   300   600   900   1200 Yds
0   300   600   900   1200 M
```

Circus of Nero

SEVEN HILLS OF ROME

I Quirinal
II Viminal
III Esquiline
IV Caelian
V Palatine
VI Capitoline
VII Aventine

1 Basilica Julia
2 Roman Forum
3 Carcer (Mamertine Prison)
4 Forum of Julius Caesar
5 Basilica Aemilia
6 Sacred Way
7 House of Vestals
8 Palace of Caligula
9 Palace of Tiberius

Flaminian Way
Praetorian Camp
Baths of Nero
High Path
Viminal Gate
Stadium of Domitian
Broad Way
Patrician Street
Tiber River
Flaminian Circus
Forum of Augustus
Esquiline Gate
Forum of Vespasian
Servian
Gate
Flavian Amphitheater
Temple of Apollo
Palace of Augustus
Circus Maximus
Aqueduct
Capena Gate
Market
Appian Way

Roads and buildings are that of the time of Flavian, A.D. 69-96

© Copyright HAMMOND INC., Maplewood, N.J.

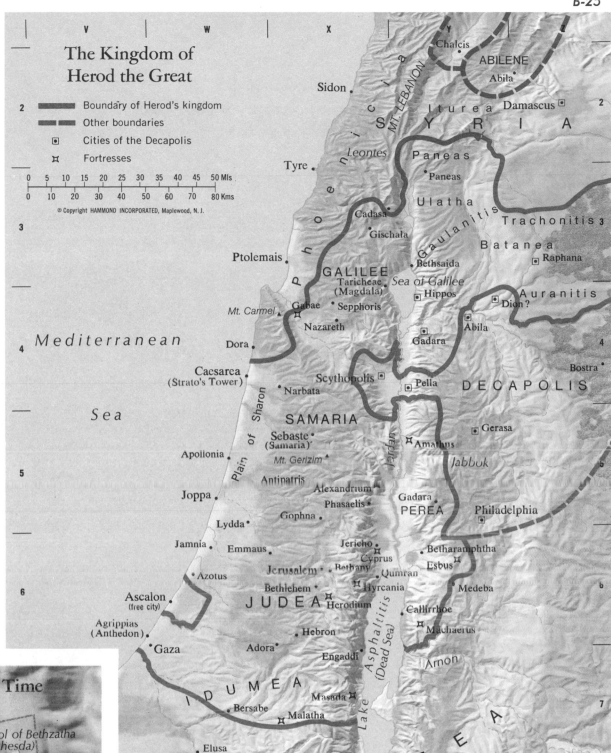

The Kingdom of Herod the Great

▬▬▬	Boundary of Herod's kingdom
▬ ▬ ▬	Other boundaries
⊡	Cities of the Decapolis
⋈	Fortresses

```
0   5  10  15  20  25  30  35  40  45  50 Mls
0   10    20    30    40    50    60    70   80 Kms
```
© Copyright HAMMOND INCORPORATED, Maplewood, N.J.

Map labels:

Caspian Sea, ha (Volga), CAUCASUS, Iberia, Albania, Artaxata, ARMENIA, PARTHIAN EMPIRE, Tigris, Euphrates, Ctesiphon, Arabia, Mediterranean Sea

Chalcis, ABILENE, Abila, Sidon, SYRIA, MT. LEBANON, Iturea, Damascus ⊡, Tyre, Leontes, Paneas, Paneas, Ulatha, Cadasa, Gischala, Gaulanitis, Trachonitis, Batanea, Raphana ⊡, Ptolemais, GALILEE, Bethsaida, Auranitis, Taricheae (Magdala), Sea of Galilee, Hippos ⊡, Dion ? ⊡, Mt. Carmel, Gabae ⋈, Sepphoris, Nazareth, Abila, Gadara, Dora, Caesarea (Strato's Tower), Scythopolis ⊡, Pella ⊡, DECAPOLIS, Narbata, Bostra, SAMARIA, Sebaste (Samaria), Amathus ⋈, Gerasa ⊡, Apollonia, Mt. Gerizim, Jabbok, Antipatris, Joppa, Alexandrium ⋈, Gadara, Phasaelis, Philadelphia ⊡, Lydda, Gophna, PEREA, Jamnia, Emmaus, Jericho ⋈, Betharamphtha, Cyprus ⋈, Esbus, Azotus, Jerusalem, Bethany, Qumran, Medeba, Ascalon (free city), Bethlehem, Hyrcania ⋈, Agrippias (Anthedon), Herodium ⋈, Callirrhoe ⋈, Gaza, Hebron, Adora, Engaddi, Arnon, JUDEA, Asphaltitis (Dead Sea), Machaerus ⋈, IDUMEA, Masada ⋈, Bersabe, Malatha ⋈, NABATEA, Elusa, Khirbet Tannur Nabatean sanctuary, Nessana

Plain of Sharon, Phoenicia, Jordan, Lake Asphaltitis (Dead Sea)

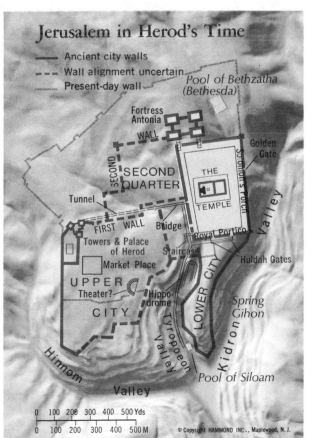

Jerusalem in Herod's Time

——	Ancient city walls
– – –	Wall alignment uncertain
······	Present-day wall

Pool of Bethzatha (Bethesda), Fortress Antonia, WALL, Golden Gate, SECOND QUARTER, Solomon's Porch, THE TEMPLE, Tunnel, SECOND, FIRST WALL, Bridge, Royal Portico, Towers & Palace of Herod, Staircase, Market Place, Huldah Gates, UPPER CITY, Theater?, Hippo-drome, LOWER CITY, Spring Gihon, Tyropoeon Valley, Kidron Valley, Hinnom Valley, Pool of Siloam

```
0  100  200  300  400  500 Yds
0  100  200  300  400  500 M
```
© Copyright HAMMOND INC., Maplewood, N.J.

Temple of Herod

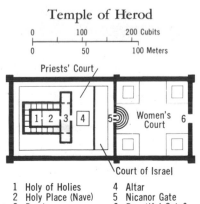

```
0       100       200 Cubits
0        50       100 Meters
```

Priests' Court, Women's Court, Court of Israel

1 Holy of Holies
2 Holy Place (Nave)
3 Porch
4 Altar
5 Nicanor Gate
6 Beautiful Gate?

Model of Herod's Temple, with surrounding courts and Royal Portico in the background.

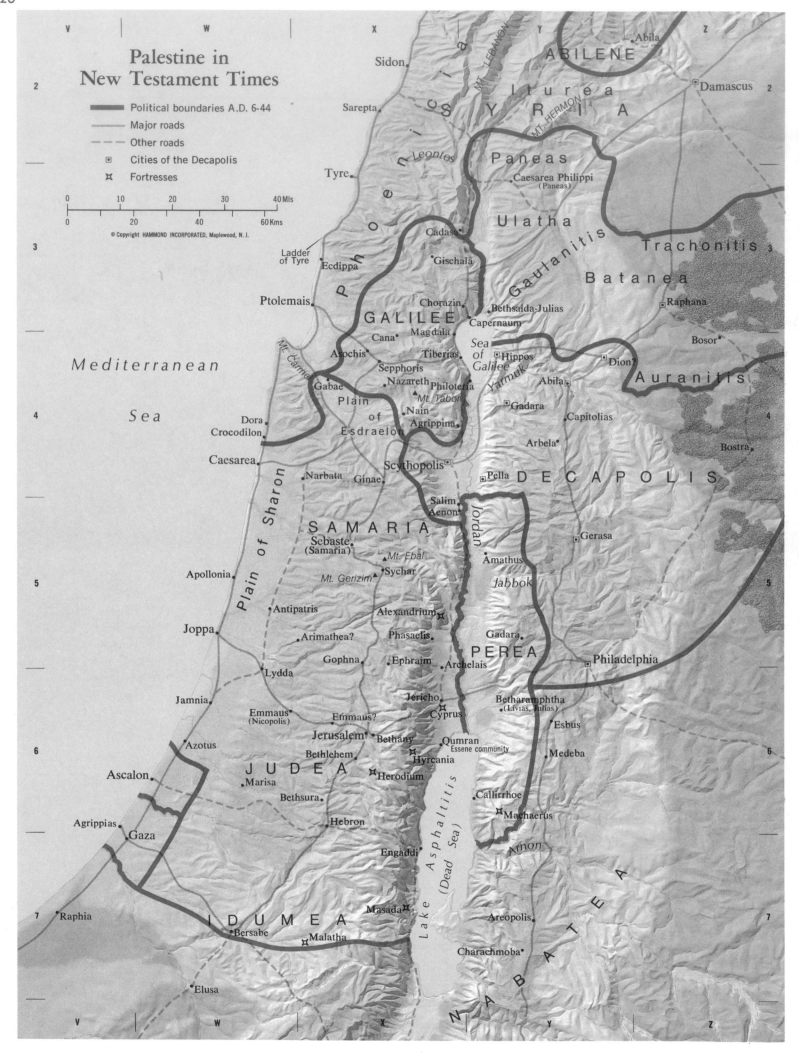

Palestine in New Testament Times

	Political boundaries A.D. 6-44
	Major roads
	Other roads
⊡	Cities of the Decapolis
⌘	Fortresses

0 10 20 30 40 Mls
0   20   40   60 Kms

© Copyright HAMMOND INCORPORATED, Maplewood, N.J.

Mediterranean

Sea

Ph o e n i c i a

SYRIA

Iturea

ABILENE

Abila

Damascus

Sidon

Sarepta

Mt. LEBANON

Mt. HERMON

Paneas

Leontes

Tyre

Ladder of Tyre

Ecdippa

Cadasa

Gischala

Caesarea Philippi (Paneas)

Ulatha

Trachonitis

Batanea

Ptolemais

Chorazin

Bethsaida-Julias

Raphana

GALILEE

Capernaum

Cana

Magdala

Sea of Galilee

Hippos

Dion?

Bosor

Asochis

Tiberias

Gaulanitis

Mt. Carmel

Sepphoris

Nazareth

Philoteria

Abila

Auranitis

Gabae

Plain of Esdraelon

Mt. Tabor

Nain

Agrippina

Yarmuk

Gadara

Capitolias

Bostra

Dora

Crocodilon

Arbela

Caesarea

Scythopolis

DECAPOLIS

Narbata

Ginae

Pella

Gerasa

Plain of Sharon

SAMARIA

Salim

Aenon

Jordan

Sebaste (Samaria)

Mt. Ebal

Amathus

Jabbok

Apollonia

Mt. Gerizim

Sychar

Antipatris

Alexandrium

Joppa

Arimathea?

Phasaelis

Gadara

PEREA

Philadelphia

Gophna

Ephraim

Archelais

Lydda

Jericho

Betharamphtha (Livias, Julias)

Jamnia

Emmaus (Nicopolis)

Emmaus?

Cyprus

Esbus

Jerusalem

Bethany

Qumran

Essene community

Medeba

Azotus

Bethlehem

Hyrcania

Ascalon

Marisa

JUDEA

Herodium

Callirrhoe

Bethsura

Machaerus

Agrippias

Gaza

Hebron

Lake Asphaltitis (Dead Sea)

Arnon

Engaddi

Areopolis

Raphia

IDUMEA

Masada

N A B A T E A

Bersabe

Malatha

Charachmoba

Elusa

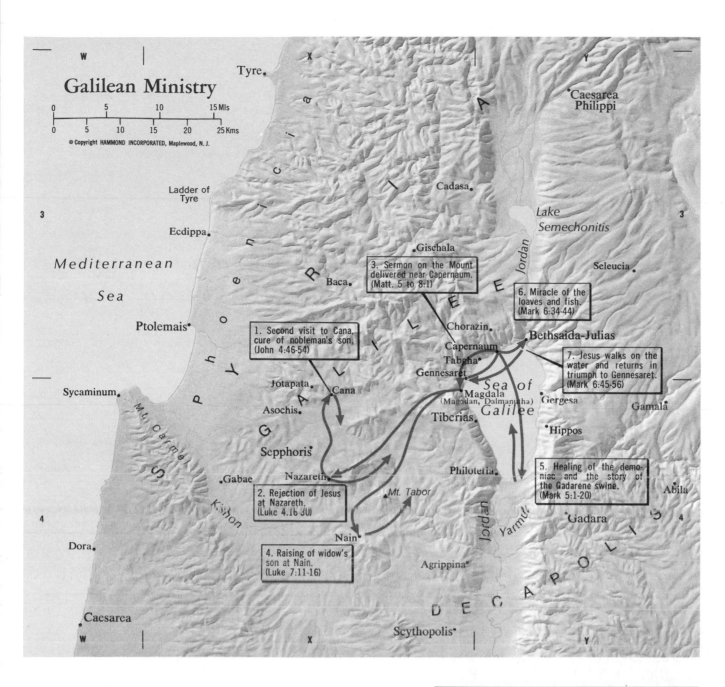

Galilean Ministry

0 5 10 15 Mls
0 5 10 15 20 25 Kms
© Copyright HAMMOND INCORPORATED, Maplewood, N. J.

Tyre

Caesarea Philippi

Cadasa

Lake Semechonitis

Ladder of Tyre

Ecdippa

Mediterranean Sea

Gischala

3. Sermon on the Mount delivered near Capernaum. (Matt. 5 to 8:1)

Baca

Seleucia

6. Miracle of the loaves and fish. (Mark 6:34-44)

Ptolemais

1. Second visit to Cana, cure of nobleman's son. (John 4:46-54)

Chorazin

Capernaum

Bethsaida-Julias

Tabgha

7. Jesus walks on the water and returns in triumph to Gennesaret. (Mark 6:45-56)

Gennesaret

Sycaminum

Jotapata

Cana

Magdala (Magadan, Dalmanutha)

Sea of Galilee

Gergesa

Gamala

Asochis

Tiberias

Sepphoris

Hippos

Gabae

Nazareth

Philoteria

5. Healing of the demoniac and the story of the Gadarene swine. (Mark 5:1-20)

Abila

2. Rejection of Jesus at Nazareth. (Luke 4:16-30)

Mt. Tabor

Gadara

Dora

Nain

Yarmuk

4. Raising of widow's son at Nain. (Luke 7:11-16)

Agrippina

Caesarea

DECAPOLIS

Scythopolis

Above the waters of the Sea of Galilee the Church of the Beatitudes dominates the hill where tradition says Jesus preached the Sermon on the Mount.

The excavated synagogue at Capernaum (right) is later than the time of Jesus, but recalls that the Galilean Ministry was based in Capernaum, where Jesus spent much time teaching and healing in the synagogue.

The traditional site of Jesus' baptism is here at the Jordan River.

Machaerus, where John the Baptist was put to death on orders of Herod Antipas.

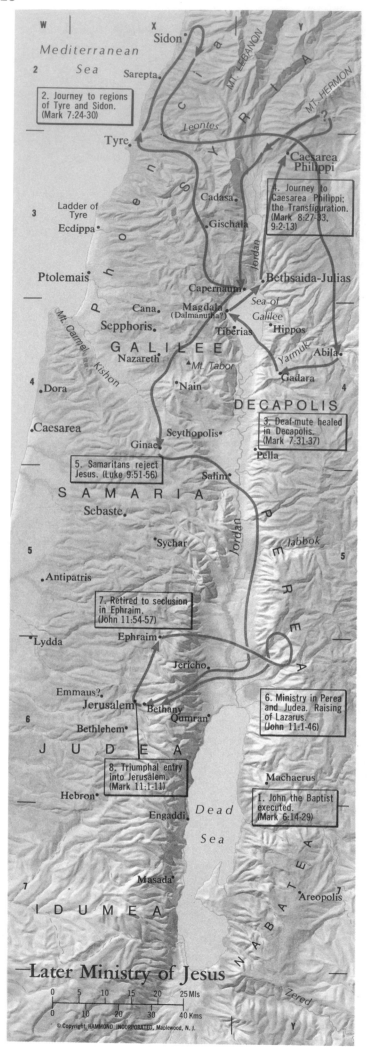

Later Ministry of Jesus

(Map labels)

Mediterranean Sea

Sidon

Sarepta

2. Journey to regions of Tyre and Sidon. (Mark 7:24-30)

MT. LEBANON

MT. HERMON

Leontes

Tyre

Caesarea Philippi

Ladder of Tyre

Cadasa

4. Journey to Caesarea Philippi; the Transfiguration. (Mark 8:27-33; 9:2-13)

Ecdippa

Gischala

Ptolemais

Bethsaida-Julias

Capernaum

Cana

Magdala (Dalmanutha?)

Sea of Galilee

Sepphoris

Tiberias

Hippos

GALILEE

Nazareth

Mt. Tabor

Abila

Yarmuk

Dora

Nain

Gadara

DECAPOLIS

Caesarea

Scythopolis

3. Deaf-mute healed in Decapolis. (Mark 7:31-37)

Ginae

Pella

5. Samaritans reject Jesus. (Luke 9:51-56)

Salim

SAMARIA

Sebaste

Jabbok

Sychar

Jordan

Antipatris

7. Retired to seclusion in Ephraim. (John 11:54-57)

Lydda

Ephraim

Jericho

Emmaus?

Jerusalem

Bethany

Qumran

6. Ministry in Perea and Judea. Raising of Lazarus. (John 11:1-46)

Bethlehem

JUDEA

8. Triumphal entry into Jerusalem. (Mark 11:1-11)

Hebron

Machaerus

1. John the Baptist executed. (Mark 6:14-29)

Engaddi

Dead Sea

Masada

Areopolis

IDUMEA

NABATAEA

Zered

0 5 10 15 20 25 Mls
0 10 20 30 40 Kms

© Copyright HAMMOND INCORPORATED, Maplewood, N.J.

The Events of Passion Week

(According to the Synoptic Gospels)

	MATT.	MARK	LUKE
SUNDAY (Palm Sunday)			
Triumphal entry into Jerusalem	21:1-9	11:1-10	19:28-44
Visit to Temple and return to Bethany	21:10-17	11:11	19:45-46
MONDAY			
On the way to Jerusalem Jesus curses an unfruitful fig tree	21:18-19	11:12-14	
The Temple court cleansed		11:15-19	19:45-48
TUESDAY			
Returning to Jerusalem, Jesus explains the withering of the fig tree	21:20-22	11:20-26	
Jesus' authority is questioned	21:23-27	11:27-33	20:1-8
Teachings in the Temple	21:28-46; 22	12:1-37a	20:9-44
Condemnation of scribes and Pharisees	23:1-36	12:37b-40	20:45-47
Jesus in Temple treasury calls attention to widow's gift		12:41-44	21:1-4
Prediction of destruction of the Temple and the end of the World	24:1-44	13:1-37	21:5-38
WEDNESDAY			
Conspiracy against Jesus	26:1-5	14:1-2	22:1-2
Anointing at Bethany	26:6-13	14:1-9	
Judas agrees to betray Jesus	26:14-16	14:10-11	22:3-6
THURSDAY (Maundy Thursday)			
Jesus prepares to celebrate Passover	26:17-19	14:12-16	22:7-13
The Last Supper	26:20-29	14:17-25	22:14-38
Withdrawal to Gethsemane	26:30-46	14:26-42	22:39-46
Betrayal and arrest of Jesus	26:47-56	14:43-52	22:47-53
Jesus before Caiaphas and members of the Sanhedrin; Peter's denial	26:57-75	14:53-72	22:54-71
FRIDAY (Good Friday)			
Trial before Pilate; Judas' suicide	27:1-2	15:1-5	23:1-5
Jesus sent to Herod			23:6-16
Pilate imposes sentence of death	27:15-26	15:6-15	23:17-25
Jesus scourged and led to Golgotha	27:27-32	15:15-21	
Jesus' crucifixion and death	27:33-56	15:22-41	23:33-49
Jesus is buried	27:57-61	15:42-47	23:50-56
SATURDAY			
The guarded tomb	27:62-66		
SUNDAY (Easter)			
The empty tomb and the risen Christ	28:1-10	16:1-8	24:1-12

A modern church at ancient Bethany marks the traditional place where Jesus raised Lazarus from the dead (John 11:1-44).

Silver denarius of Tiberius, "tribute money" of Luke 20:21-26.

At Caesarea, residence of the Roman governors, archaeologists found this dedication stone with the only known inscriptional reference to Pontius Pilate.

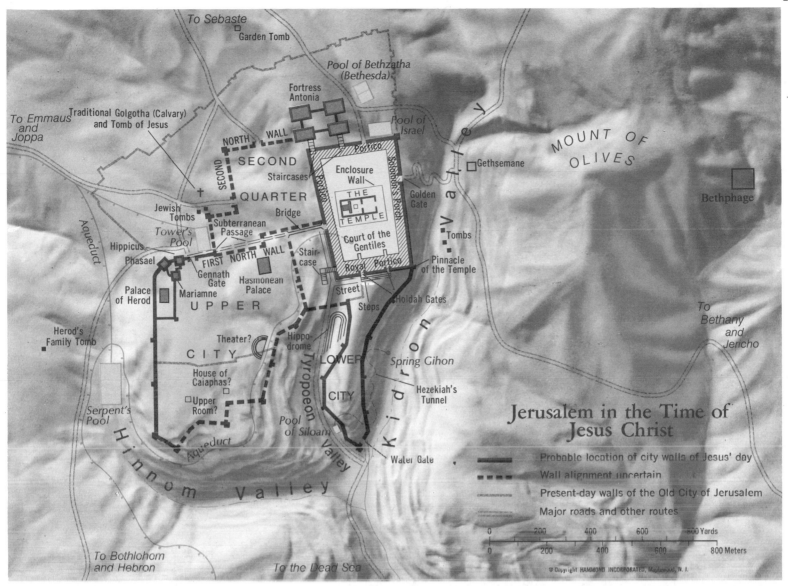

Jerusalem in the Time of Jesus Christ

Probable location of city walls of Jesus' day
Wall alignment uncertain
Present-day walls of the Old City of Jerusalem
Major roads and other routes

Today a mosque, the magnificent Dome of the Rock, occupies the platform where Herod's Temple stood in Jesus' day.

Judas' 30 pieces of silver may have been Tyrian shekels of this type.

A model of Jerusalem shows the Temple platform and four towers of Fortress Antonia. The Pool of Bethzatha where Jesus healed the crippled man is the square-shaped building with reddish roof in the foreground.

The Garden Tomb, a rock-cut tomb of the type in which Jesus was buried. North of Jerusalem, this quiet spot just outside the present north wall is a rival to the traditional site of the crucifixion and burial.

"The Pavement" (courtyard) of the Fortress Antonia was possibly the place where Jesus was tried by Pilate. Today it is the crypt of a church and convent.

Theodotus synagogue inscription found on Mount Zion in Jerusalem. Some think this dedicatory inscription refers to the "Synagogue of the Freedmen" mentioned in Acts 6:9.

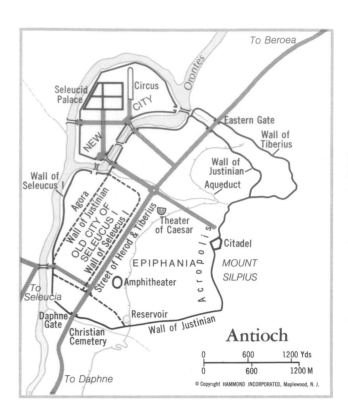

Antioch

The Lion Gate in Jerusalem's east wall. Medieval Christian tradition locates the martyrdom of Stephen (Acts 7:58-60) nearby. Therefore Christians call this "St. Stephen's Gate."

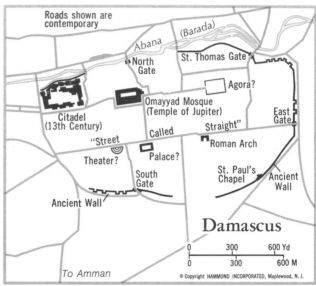

Damascus

St. Paul's Chapel, Damascus. This is the traditional location of Paul's escape over the city wall (Acts 9:25).

The theater by the sea at Caesarea where in 10 B.C. Herod dedicated his splendid new city. Now restored, it is used for concerts.

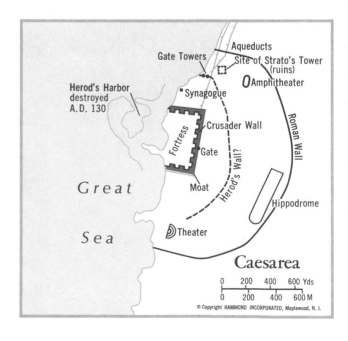

Caesarea

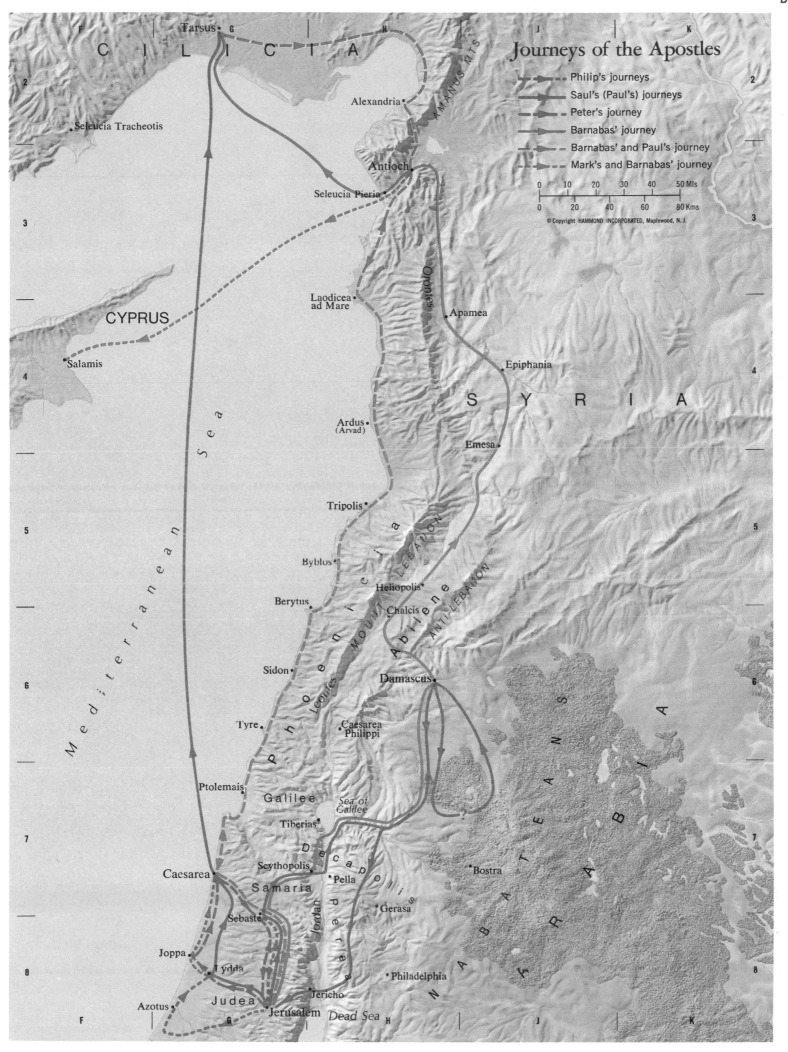

Journeys of the Apostles

- - - - ► Philip's journeys
———► Saul's (Paul's) journeys
- - - ► Peter's journey
———► Barnabas' journey
- - - ► Barnabas' and Paul's journey
- - - ► Mark's and Barnabas' journey

0   10   20   30   40   50 Mls
0   20   40   60   80 Kms
© Copyright HAMMOND INCORPORATED, Maplewood, N.J.

CILICIA

Tarsus

Seleucia Tracheotis

Alexandria

AMANUS MTS

Antioch

Seleucia Pieria

CYPRUS

Salamis

Mediterranean Sea

Laodicea ad Mare

Apamea

Orontes

SYRIA

Epiphania

Ardus (Arvad)

Emesa

Tripolis

Byblos

LEBANON

Heliopolis

Berytus

Chalcis

Abilene

ANTI-LEBANON

Leontes

MOUNT LEBANON

Phoenicia

Sidon

Damascus

Tyre

Caesarea Philippi

Ptolemais

Galilee

Sea of Galilee

Tiberias

Decapolis

Scythopolis

Pella

Caesarea

Samaria

Gerasa

Bostra

Sebaste

Jordan

Perea

NABATEAN

ARABIA

Joppa

Lydda

Philadelphia

Azotus

Judea

Jericho

Jerusalem

Dead Sea

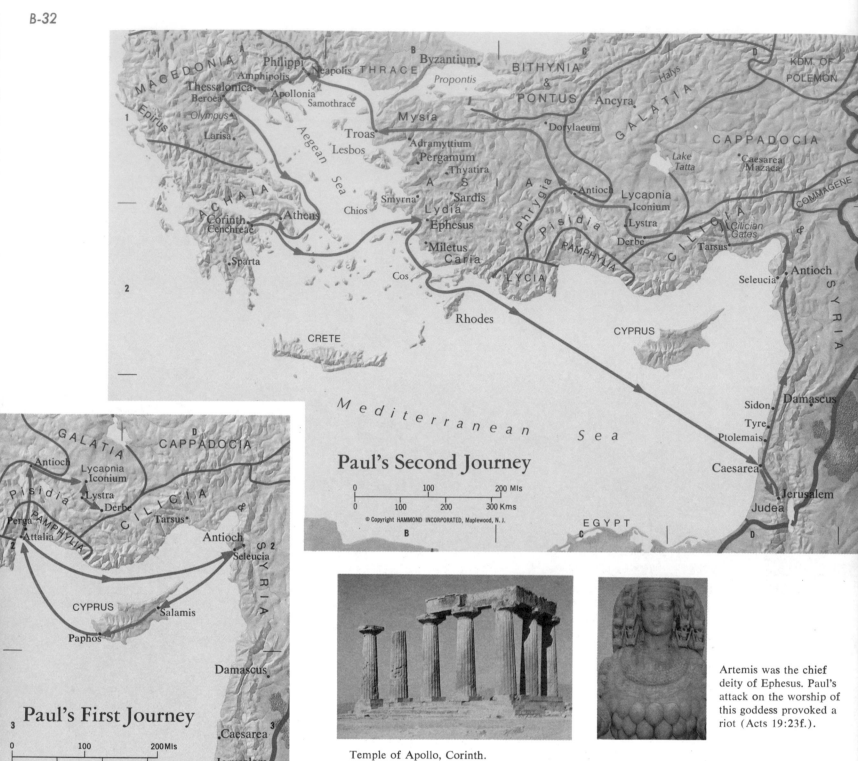

Paul's Second Journey

0   100   200 MIs

0   100   200   300 Kms

© Copyright HAMMOND INCORPORATED, Maplewood, N. J.

Paul's First Journey

0   100   200 MIs

0   100   200   300 Kms

© Copyright HAMMOND INCORPORATED, Maplewood, N. J.

Artemis was the chief deity of Ephesus. Paul's attack on the worship of this goddess provoked a riot (Acts 19:23f.).

Temple of Apollo, Corinth. Only 7 of the 38 columns seen by Paul are now standing.

The Acropolis rises behind the Areopagus (foreground) where Paul was mocked by the Athenian elders (Acts 17:32).

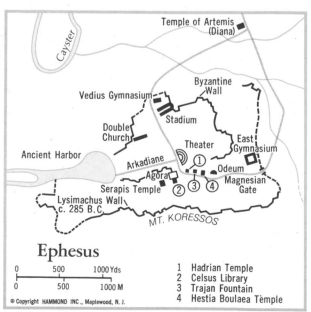

Ephesus

0   500   1000 Yds

0   500   1000 M

© Copyright HAMMOND INC., Maplewood, N. J.

1 Hadrian Temple
2 Celsus Library
3 Trajan Fountain
4 Hestia Boulaea Tèmple

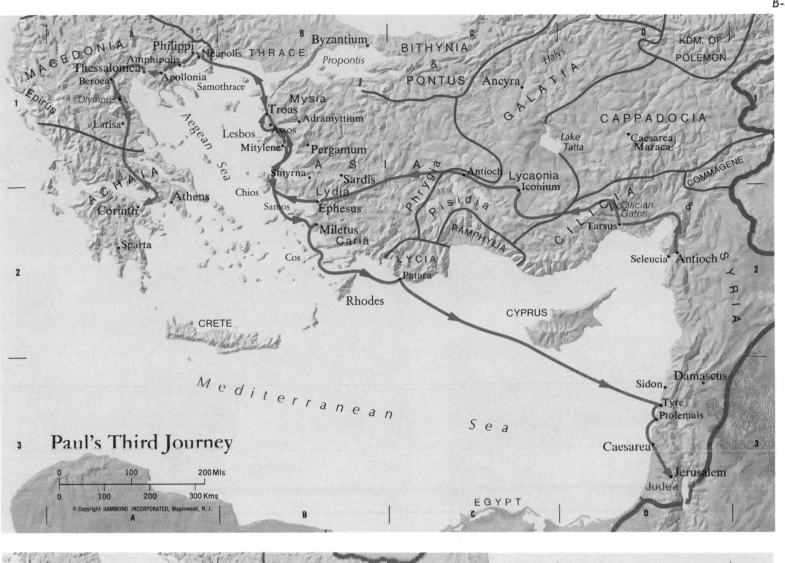

Paul's Third Journey

MACEDONIA
Philippi
Neapolis THRACE
Amphipolis
Thessalonica
Beroea
Apollonia
Samothrace
Olympus
Epirus
Larisa
Mysia
Troas
Adramyttium
Lesbos
Assos
Mitylene
Pergamum
Smyrna
Sardis
Chios
Lydia
Samos
Ephesus
Miletus
Caria
Cos
Athens
Corinth
Sparta
Aegean Sea
ACHAIA
Rhodes
Patara
LYCIA
CRETE
PAMPHYLIA
Pisidia
Phrygia
ASIA
Antioch
Lycaonia
Iconium
BITHYNIA & PONTUS
Byzantium
Propontis
Ancyra
GALATIA
Halys
Lake Tatta
CAPPADOCIA
Caesarea Mazaca
COMMAGENE
Cilician Gates
CILICIA
Tarsus
KDM. OF POLEMON
Seleucia
Antioch
SYRIA
Sidon
Damascus
Tyre
Ptolemais
Caesarea
Jerusalem
Judea
CYPRUS
Mediterranean Sea
EGYPT

0   100   200 MIs
0   100   200   300 Kms
© Copyright HAMMOND INCORPORATED, Maplewood, N.J.

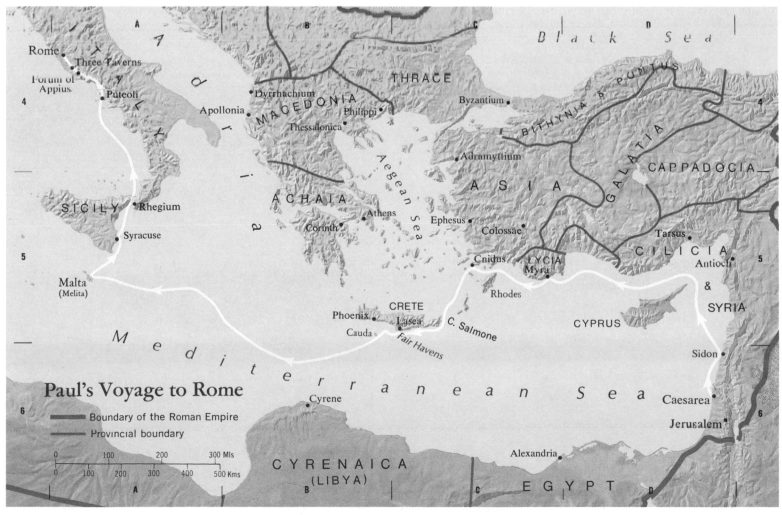

Paul's Voyage to Rome

Rome
Three Taverns
Forum of Appius
Puteoli
Adriatica
SICILY
Rhegium
Syracuse
Malta (Melita)
Dyrrhachium
MACEDONIA
Apollonia
Thessalonica
Philippi
ACHAIA
Corinth
Athens
Aegean Sea
THRACE
Byzantium
BITHYNIA & PONTUS
Black Sea
Adramyttium
ASIA
GALATIA
CAPPADOCIA
Ephesus
Colossae
Cnidus
LYCIA
Myra
Rhodes
Tarsus
CILICIA
Antioch
& SYRIA
CYPRUS
Phoenix
CRETE
Lasea
Cauda
Fair Havens
C. Salmone
Sidon
Caesarea
Jerusalem
Cyrene
Alexandria
Mediterranean Sea
CYRENAICA (LIBYA)
EGYPT

Boundary of the Roman Empire
Provincial boundary

0   100   200   300 MIs
0   100   200   300   400   500 Kms

A Roman eagle
on an altar
in Jerusalem.

Masada from the north showing the archaeologically
recovered fortress of Herod. Behind the imperial apartments
is a bathhouse surrounded by storerooms.

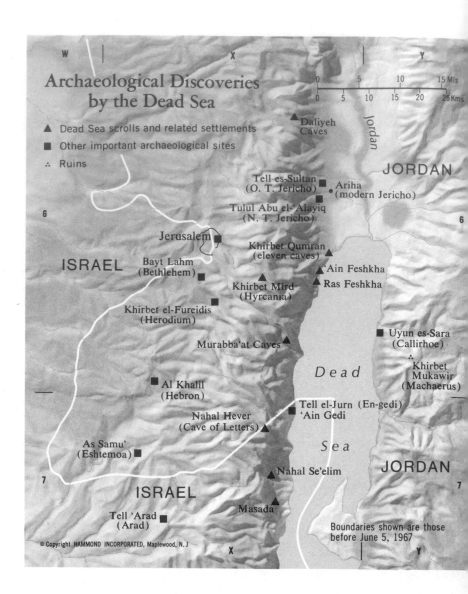

Archaeological Discoveries by the Dead Sea

▲ Dead Sea scrolls and related settlements
■ Other important archaeological sites
∴ Ruins

JORDAN

Daliyeh Caves

Tell es-Sultan (O. T. Jericho)   Ariha (modern Jericho)

Tulul Abu el-'Alayiq (N. T. Jericho)

Jerusalem   Khirbet Qumran (eleven caves)   'Ain Feshkha

ISRAEL   Bayt Lahm (Bethlehem)   Ras Feshkha

Khirbet Mird (Hyrcania)

Khirbet el-Fureidis (Herodium)

Uyun es-Sara (Callirhoe)

Murabba'at Caves   Dead   Khirbet Mukawir (Machaerus)

Al Khalil (Hebron)

Tell el-Jurn (En-gedi) 'Ain Gedi

Nahal Hever (Cave of Letters)   Sea   JORDAN

As Samu' (Eshtemoa)

Nahal Se'elim

ISRAEL   Masada

Tell 'Arad (Arad)   Boundaries shown are those before June 5, 1967

© Copyright HAMMOND INCORPORATED, Maplewood, N.J

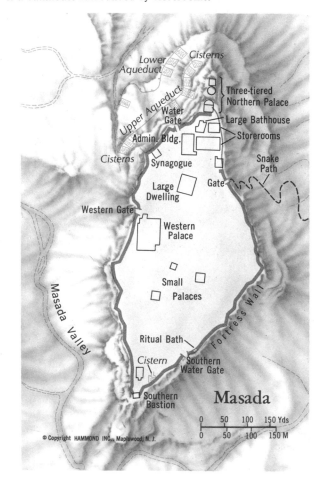

Lower Aqueduct   Cisterns

Upper Aqueduct   Water Gate   Three-tiered Northern Palace

Admin. Bldg.   Large Bathhouse

Cisterns   Storerooms

Synagogue   Snake Path

Large Dwelling   Gate

Western Gate

Western Palace

Small Palaces

Ritual Bath

Masada Valley   Fortress Wall

Cistern   Southern Water Gate

Southern Bastion   ## Masada

0   50   100   150 Yds

0   50   100   150 M

© Copyright HAMMOND INC., Maplewood, N. J.

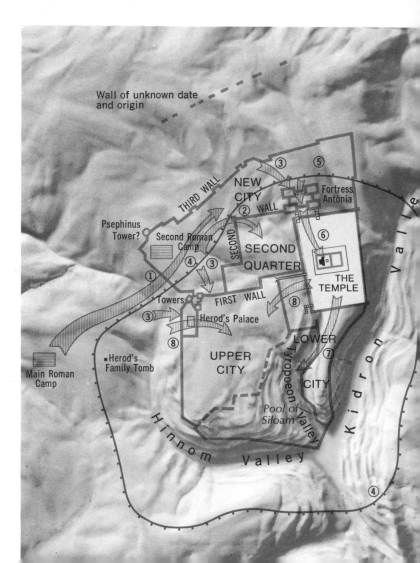

Wall of unknown date and origin

THIRD WALL   NEW CITY   ③   ⑤

Fortress Antonia

Psephinus Tower?   ②   WALL

Second Roman Camp   SECOND

⑥

④   ③   SECOND QUARTER   THE TEMPLE

①   FIRST WALL   ⑧

Towers

③   Herod's Palace   LOWER

⑧   ⑦

Main Roman Camp   Herod's Family Tomb   UPPER CITY   CITY

Pool of Siloam

Hinnom   Valley   Tyropoeon Valley   Kidron Valley

④

Copper Scrolls found at Qumran.

Cave Four at Qumran (center) in which a wealth of precious scrolls were found.

The Siege of Jerusalem
A.D. 70

```
0    200   400   600   800 Yards
0    200   400   600   800 Meters
```
© Copyright HAMMOND INCORPORATED, Maplewood, N. J.

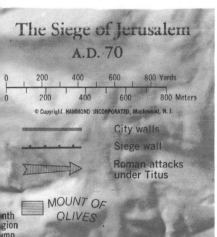

- ——— City walls
- ········ Siege wall
- ▷ Roman attacks under Titus
- ▨ MOUNT OF OLIVES
- nth gion mp

① Romans breach Third Wall May 25 and capture New City.
② Romans enter Second Quarter. Jews withdraw behind First Wall. May 30-June 2.
③ Titus' divided attack on First Wall and the Antonia fails.
④ Romans build siege wall around city.
⑤ Romans renew assault on the Antonia. Fortress falls to Titus July 22.
⑥ Romans burn gates and enter Temple courtyards. On August 29 Temple destroyed by fire.
⑦ Romans burn Lower City. September 2?
⑧ Romans assault Herod's Palace and enter the Upper City. Resistance ends on September 26.

The First Jewish Revolt

- •••••• Border of areas in revolt A.D. 66
- ☐ Area lost by Jews in 67
- ☐ Area lost by Jews in 68
- ☐ Remaining Jewish strongholds given up to Romans 70-73
- ☼ Roman siege
- 71 Dates of Roman campaigns
- ⟶ Under Gallus 66
- ⤍ Under Vespasian 66-68
- ⋯▸ Under Titus 70
- •••▸ Under Bassus 71
- ∘∘∘▸ Under Silva 73

```
0    5    10   15   20   25 Mls
0    10   20   30   40 Kms
```
© Copyright HAMMOND INCORPORATED, Maplewood, N. J.

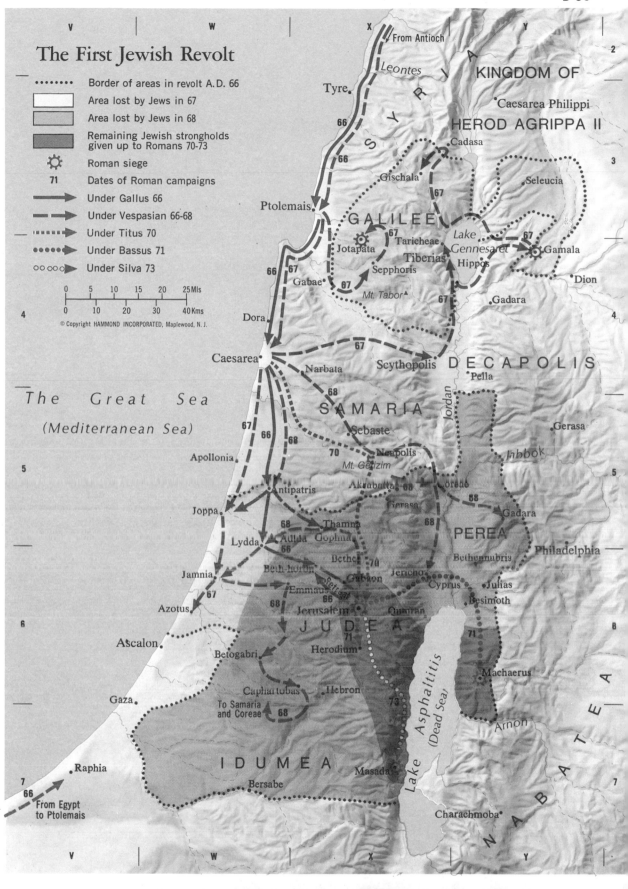

The Great Sea
(Mediterranean Sea)

Silver shekel from the "year three," the third year of the Revolt (A.D. 68).

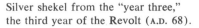

Roman "Judaea Capta" coins. Above are Vespasian and Titus. Sestertius, right, shows a captive Jewess.

GERMANIA

Cologne

Trier

Rhine

Danube

GAUL

Lugdunum
(Lyons)
Vienne

Astorga
Leon

SPAIN

Saragossa

Merida

Hispalis
Corduba

ILLYRICUM
Salona

ITALY

Ostia Rome
Antium
Puteoli

MACEDONIA
Beroea Thessalo
Larissa
Nicopolis
ACHAIA
Patrae
Corinth
Sparta

Mediterranean

Sicily
Syracuse

MAURETANIA

Sitifi Cirta
Thuburba Carthage
Lambesis Uthina
Madaurus
Numidia Hadrumetum
Thysdrus

AFRICA

Gort

Cyrene

CYRENAICA

The Spread of Christianity

- The Seven Churches of Asia (Rev. 1-3)
- City with Christian church recorded in second century
- Regions known to contain Christians by A.D. 185 (the time of Irenaeus)
- Boundary of the Roman empire for most of second century
- Temporarily controlled by Rome

0   100   200   300   400   500 Mls
0   200   400   600   800 Kms

© Copyright HAMMOND INCORPORATED, Maplewood, N.J.

St. Paul's-Outside-the-Walls, Rome, traditional site of the tomb of Paul.

The Flavian Amphitheater (Colosseum) in Rome, where many Christians were martyred.

Constantine made Christianity a "legal religion" in A.D. 311.

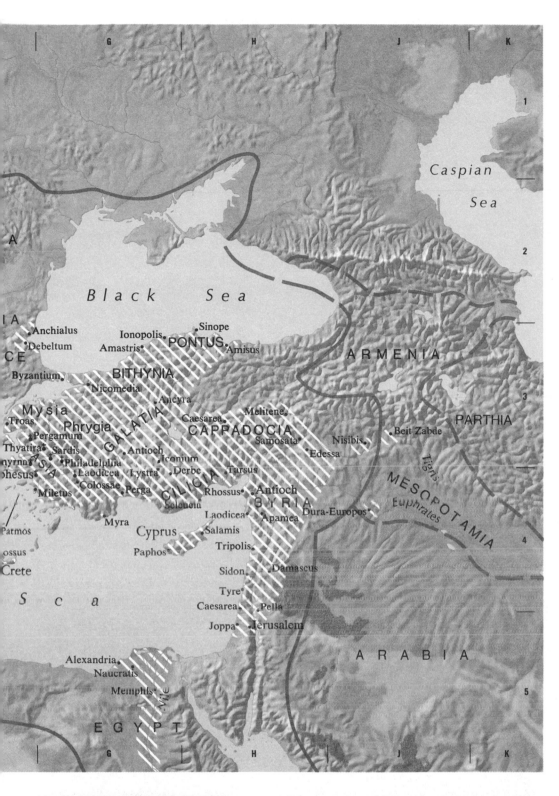

Limestone statuette of Coptic Christian woman with cross, from 4th-century A.D. Egypt.

Chalice of Antioch shows Christ and apostles. It dates from 4th or 5th century A.D.

Patmos, where The Revelation to St. John the Divine, the last book in the New Testament, was written.

Papyrus fragment of the Gospel of Matthew from Qxyrhynchus, Egypt.

Lid of Philistine anthropoid coffin from Beth-shan.

The Moabite Stone, found in 1868 at Mesha's capital. Carved about 840-820 B.C., it tells of the events of 2 Kings 3:4-27 and their aftermath from a Moabite point of view.

The mound of Tell el-Hesi. One of the first sites to be excavated in Palestine, it is thought to be Biblical Eglon, a Canaanite royal city taken by Joshua (Joshua 10).

Archaeological Sites
in Israel and Jordan

- Prehistoric cave sites
- Major excavated sites
- Other important excavations

0 5 10 15 20 25 Mls
0 10 20 30 40 Kms

© Copyright HAMMOND INCORPORATED, Maplewood, N.J.

This four-spouted lamp is from Patriarchal times.

A footed lamp from the period of the Hebrew kings.

Jesus knew this type of Herodian lamp.

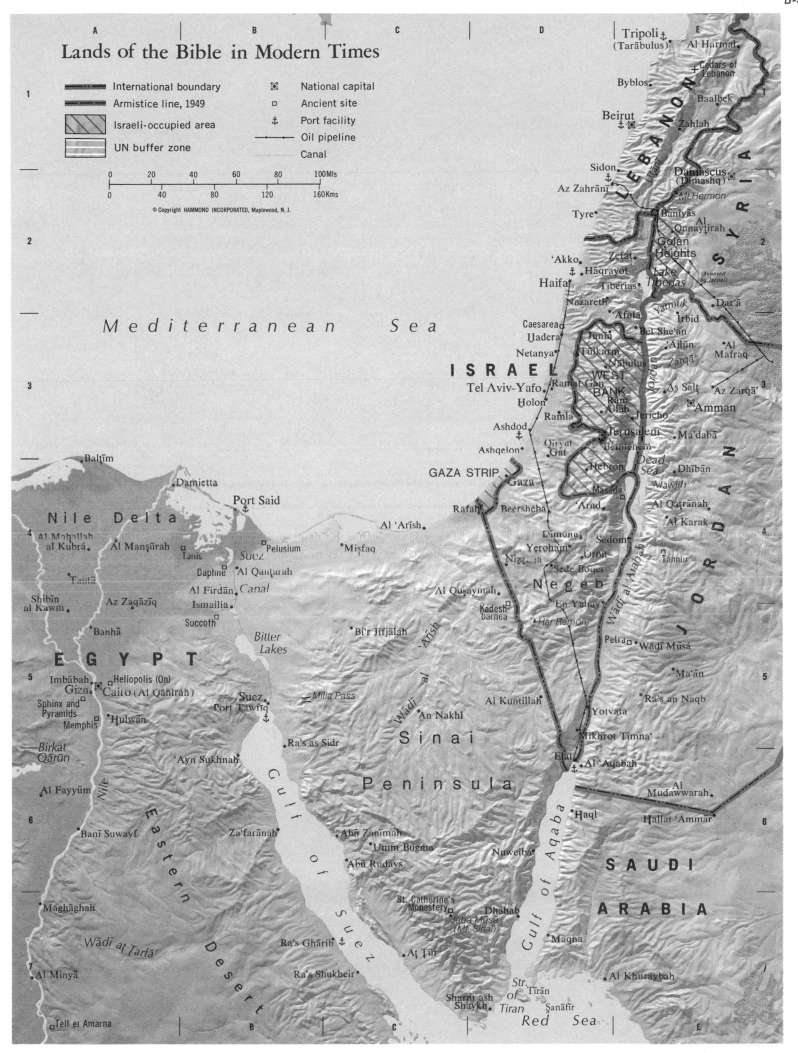

Lands of the Bible in Modern Times

International boundary
Armistice line, 1949
Israeli-occupied area
UN buffer zone

National capital
Ancient site
Port facility
Oil pipeline
Canal

0 20 40 60 80 100Mls
0 40 80 120 160Kms

© Copyright HAMMOND INCORPORATED, Maplewood, N.J.

Tripoli
(Tarābulus)
Al Harmal
Cedars of
Lebanon
Byblos
Baalbek
LEBANON
Beirut
Zahlah
Sidon
Damascus
(Dimashq)
Az Zahrānī
Mt. Hermon
SYRIA
Tyre
Baniyās
Al
Qunayṭirah
Golan
Heights
'Akko
Ḥaqrayot
(Annexed
by Israel)
Haifa
Zefat
Lake
Tiberias
Tiberias
Nazareth
Yarmuk
Dar'ā
Caesarea
Afula
Irbid
Ḥadera
Junin
Bet She'an
Ajlūn
Al
Mafraq
Netanya
Tūlkarm
Zarqā'
Nābulus
ISRAEL
WEST
As Salt
Tel Aviv-Yafo
Ramat Gan
BANK
Az Zarqā'
Holon
Ram
Allah
Amman
Ramla
Jericho
Ashdod
Jerusalem
Ma'daba
Ashqelon
Qiryat
Gat
Bethlehem
Dead
Sea
Dhībān
GAZA STRIP
Hebron
Gaza
Masada
Mawjib
Al Qatrānah
Rafah
Beersheba
Arad
Al Karak
Dimona
JORDAN
Sedom
Yeroham
Negeb
Oron
Tannur
Nizzana
Sede Boqer
Al Qusaymah
En Yahav
Kadesh-
barnea
Har Ramon
Petra
Wādī Mūsā
Ma'ān
Al Kuntillah
Ra's an Naqb
Yotvata
Mikhrot Timna'
Elat
Al 'Aqabah
Al
Mudawwarah
Ḥaql
Hallat 'Ammar

M e d i t e r r a n e a n   S e a

Balṭīm
Damietta
Port Said
Nile Delta
Al Maḥallah
al Kubrā
Al Manṣūrah
Tanta
Pelusium
Al 'Arīsh
Mīsfaq
Suez
Daphne
Al Qanṭarah
Tanta
Al Firdān
Canal
Shibīn
al Kawm
Az Zaqāzīq
Ismailia
Banhā
Succoth
Bi'r Jifjālah
Bitter
Lakes
EGYPT
Imbābah
Heliopolis (On)
Giza
Cairo (Al Qahirah)
Sphinx and
Pyramids
Memphis
Ḥulwān
Suez
Port Tawfīq
Mitla Pass
An Nakhl
Al Kuntillah
Birkat
Qārūn
Ra's as Sidr
Wādī
al
'Arīsh
Sinai
Al Fayyūm
'Ayn Sukhnah
Peninsula
Gulf of Aqaba
Bani Suwayf
Za'farānah
Abū Zanīmah
SAUDI
Umm Bugma
Nuweiba'
Maghāghah
Abū Rudays
ARABIA
Eastern
Desert
Gulf of Suez
St. Catherine's
Monastery
Dhahab
Jabal Mūsā
(Mt. Sinai)
Maqna
Nile
Wādī aṭ Ṭarfā'
Ra's Ghārib
Aṭ Ṭūr
Al Khuraybah
Al Minyā
Ra's Shukheir
Str.
of
Tiran
Tiran
Sharm ash
Shaykh
Ṣanāfir
Red
Sea
Tell el Amarna

Time Chart of Bible History

DATE	PALESTINE	EGYPT	MESOPOTAMIA & PERSIA	ANATOLIA & SYRIA	GREECE & ROME
4000 BC	Neolithic culture (Jericho)	— First use of metal: copper and bronze —			
	Ghassulian culture c.3500	Hieroglyphic writing developed	Halaf culture Cuneiform writing developed		
	The Canaanites, a Semitic people, were ancestral to the Phoenicians	**Archaic Period** Menes unifies Egypt	Sumerian city states c.2800-2360	Early Bronze cities Byblos, Troy, Ugarit	
	Early Bronze urban culture c.3300	**Old Kingdom** The Great Pyramids at Gizeh c.2550	**Akkadian Empire** Sargon I 2360-2305	Syria under Akkadian Empire	Beginning of Minoan civilization on Crete
	Amorite invasions c.2500-2300	Old Kingdom falls	Gutian kings Ur dominance	Hittites enter Anatolia	Greeks invade Balkan peninsula
2000 BC			Ur falls c.1950	Amorite invasions	
	Egypt controls Canaan	**Middle Kingdom**	**Isin-Larsa Period** **Old Babylonian Empire**	Hittites intro. Iron	**Minoan Sea Empire**
	Abraham — oral tradition	Hyksos invaders from Asia c.1720-1550	Hammurabi 1728-1686	Labarnas I c.1600	
	Israelite sojourn in Egypt	**New Kingdom**	**Kassite Period** Hittites sack Babylon 1531	**Old Hittite Kingdom**	Mycenae shaft graves
	Battle of Megiddo 1468 Amarna letters c.1370-1353	Akhenaton 1370-1353 Tutankhamen 1353-1344	Mitanni Kdm.	Mursilis I c.1540	Cretan palaces destroyed c.1400
	The Exodus c.1290 Israelite invasion	Ramses II 1290-1224 Ramses III defeats Sea Peoples c.1170	**Rise of Assyria** Shalmaneser I	Suppilullumas **Hittite Empire**	Dorians invade Greece
	Philistine penetration Kdm. of Saul c.1020-1000	**Late Dynastic Period**	Tiglath-pileser I 1115-1078	Battle of Kedesh 1296 Sack of Troy 1192	Trojan War c.1200
1000 BC	**United Kingdom**			Arameans flood into Syria	Decline of Aegean Bronze Age civilization
	David c.1000-961 Solomon c.961-922	Period of decline		Hiram of Tyre 969-936	
	First Temple completed c.950	Shishak c.935-914	**Assyrian Empire**	Damascus city state	Latins settle in central Italy
	Divided Kingdom Rehoboam & Jeroboam I	Libyan dynasties 950-710	Asshurnasirpal II 883-859	Ben-hadad II	
	Omri dynasty 876-842 Samaria founded c.875		Shalmaneser III 859-824	Battle of Qarqar 853	
	Jehu dynasty 842-745		Adad-nirari III 807-782	Phoenicians found Carthage 814	
800 BC	Israel resurgence under Jeroboam II 786-746 Amos, Hosea Fall of Samaria and exile of Israel 722/721		Tiglath-pileser III 745-727		First Olympics 776 Legendary founding of Rome 753
	Hezekiah of Judah 715-687/6	Nubian dynasties 715-663	Sargon II 722-705 Sennacherib 705-681	Phrygian Kdm. Midas c.715	Etruscan period Homer
	Isaiah Micah Judah resurgence under Josiah 640-609 Jeremiah	Egypt under Assyrian rule 671-652 Thebes sacked 663 Neco II 609-593	Asshurbanapal 669-633 Rise of Babylon under Nabopolassar Fall of Nineveh to Medes and Babylonians 612	Lydian Kdm. Gyges of Lydia 680-652	Draco codifies Athenian law 621
600 BC					

Kings of Judah and Israel

JUDAH	ISRAEL	JUDAH	ISRAEL
Rehoboam 922-915 ●	● 922-901 Jeroboam I	Jotham 750-735 ●	● 746-745 Zechariah
Abijah 915-913 ●	● 901-900 Nadab		● 745 Shallum
Asa 913-873 ●	● 900-877 Baasha		● 745-738 Menahem
	● 877-876 Elah		● 738-737 Pekahiah
	● 876 Zimri	Ahaz 735-715 ●	● 737-732 Pekah
Jehoshaphat 873-849 ●	● 876-869 Omri		● 732-724 Hoshea
	● 869-850 Ahab	Hezekiah 715-687/6 ●	
	● 850-849 Ahaziah	Manasseh 687/6-642 ●	
Jehoram 849-842 ●	● 849-842 Jehoram	Amon 642-640 ●	
Ahaziah 842 ●	● 842-815 Jehu	Josiah 640-609 ●	
Athaliah 842-837 ●		Jehoahaz 609 ●	
Joash 837-800 ●	● 815-801 Jehoahaz	Jehoiakim 609-598 ●	
Amaziah 800-783 ●	● 801-786 Jehoash	Jehoiachin 598-597 ●	
Uzziah 783-742 ●	● 786-746 Jeroboam II	Zedekiah 597-587 ●	

DATE	PALESTINE	EGYPT	MESOPOTAMIA & PERSIA	ANATOLIA & SYRIA	GREECE & ROME
600 BC	Destruction of Jerusalem and exile of Judah 587 Ezekiel **Babylonian Captivity** Edict of Cyrus allows return of Jews 538 Zerubbabel Temple rebuilt 520-515 **Persian Period** Ezra's mission 458?? Nehemiah comes to Judah 445 (440?)	Egypt under Persian rule 525-401 Unsuccessful revolt Return to native rule	**New Babylonian Empire** Nebuchadnezzar II 605-562 **Persian Empire** Cyrus 550-530 Babylon falls 539 Cambyses 530-522 Darius I 522-486 Xerxes I 486-465 Artaxerxes I Darius II 433-404	Syria and Anatolia under Persian rule Phoenicians provide fleet for Persian attacks on Greece	Solon's judicial reforms c.590 Rome ruled by Etruscan kings Roman Republic established 509 Persian Wars 499-479 Thermopylae-Salamis 480 Pericles 461-429 Herodotus
400 BC	Ezra's mission 398? Palestine passes under Alexander's rule and Hellenization begins 332 Ptolemaic Egyptian rule 312	Persian rule 342-332 Alexander conquers Egypt 332 Ptolemy I 323-284 **Ptolemaic Kingdom** Alexandrian Jews translate Pentateuch into Greek Ptolemy V 203-181	Artaxerxes III 358-338 Alexander invades Persia 331 Seleucid rule Parthians and Bactrians gain independence c.250	Alexander takes Tyre 332 Seleucid rule Seleucus I 312-280 **Seleucid Empire** Antiochus I 280-261 Seleucus II 246-226 Antiochus III (The Great) 223-187	Socrates' death Sack of Rome by Gauls Philip II of Macedon Alexander the Great 336-323 **Alexander's Empire** Wars of the Diodochi 1st and 2nd Punic Wars Hannibal in Italy 218
200 BC	Palestine comes under Seleucid Syrian control 198 **Maccabean Period** Judas Maccabeus leads revolt of Jews 166-160 Temple rededicated 164 Jonathan 160-142 Simon 142-134 John Hyrcanus I 134-104 Aristobulus I 104-103	Ptolemy VI 181-140 Antiochus IV campaigns in Egypt Ptolemy VII 146-116	**Parthian Empire** Mithridates I 171-138 Mithridates II 124-88	Battle of Magnesia 190 Antiochus IV (Epiphanes) 175-163 Antiochus V 163-162 Demetrius I 162-150 Demetrius II 145-139 Tyre independent	Spain annexed by Rome **Empire of the Roman Republic** 3rd Punic War Romans destroy Carthage and Corinth 146 Reforms of the Gracchi
100 BC 50 BC	Alexander Jannaeus 103-76 Alexandra 76-67 Aristobulus II 67-63 Pompey takes Jerusalem for Rome 63 Hyrcanus II, high priest 63-40 Antipater governor 55	Ptolemy VIII 116-81 Ptolemy XI 80-81 Cleopatra VII 51-30	Tigranes of Armenia Phrates III 70-57 Orodes I 57-38 War with Rome 55-38 Crassus defeated	Mithridatic Wars Antiochus XIII 68-67 Anatolia and Syria under Roman control	Sulla dictator 82-79 1st Triumvirate Pompey's campaigns in Asia 66-63 Caesar's Gallic Wars 58-51

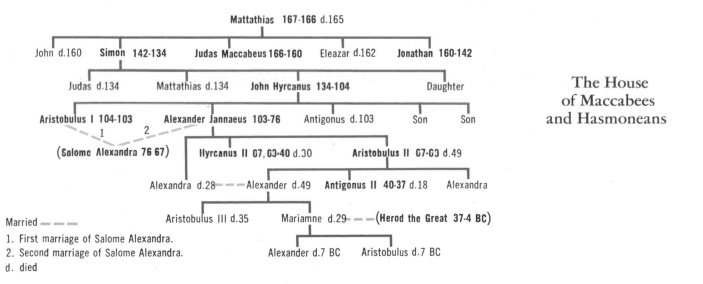

The House of Maccabees and Hasmoneans

Mattathias 167-166 d.165

John d.160 — Simon 142-134 — Judas Maccabeus 166-160 — Eleazar d.162 — Jonathan 160-142

Judas d.134 — Mattathias d.134 — John Hyrcanus 134-104 — Daughter

Aristobulus I 104-103 — Alexander Jannaeus 103-76 — Antigonus d.103 — Son — Son

1   2

(Salome Alexandra 76-67) — Hyrcanus II 67, 63-40 d.30 — Aristobulus II 67-63 d.49

Alexandra d.28 --- Alexander d.49   Antigonus II 40-37 d.18   Alexandra

Aristobulus III d.35   Mariamne d.29 --- (Herod the Great 37-4 BC)

Alexander d.7 BC   Aristobulus d.7 BC

Married - - -
1. First marriage of Salome Alexandra.
2. Second marriage of Salome Alexandra.
d. died

Time Chart of Bible History, Continued

DATE	PALESTINE	THE WEST	THE EAST
50 BC	**Roman Rule** Caesar in Judea 47 Parthian invasion 40 Antigonus 40-37 Herod the Great 37-4 BC Herod's Temple begun 18 Birth of Christ c. 4 BC Archelaus 4 BC-AD 6	Death of Pompey 48 Death of Caesar 44 2nd Triumvirate Battle of Philippi 42 Battle of Actium 31 Augustus — First emperor 27 BC-AD 14 **Roman Empire**	**Parthian Empire** Phraates 37-32 Parthians defeat Antony 36
0	Roman governors 6-41 Pontius Pilate 27-37 Death of Christ c. 29 Herod Agrippa I 41-44 Paul's 1st journey, Council at Jerusalem 46/47	Varus defeated in Germany 9 Tiberius 14-37 Gaius (Caligula) 37-41 Claudius 41-54 Conquest of Britain begun 43	Artabanus II 10-40
50 AD	Antonius Felix 52-60 Imprisonment of Paul 58 Porcius Festus 60-62 Paul sent to Rome 60 Gessius Florus 64-66 First Jewish Revolt 66-73 Destruction of Jerusalem 70 Fall of Masada 73 Jewish center at Jamnia	Nero 54-68 1st Persecution of Christians 64 Galba, Otho, Vitellius 68/69 Vespasian 69-79 Titus 79-81 Domitian 81-96 Nerva 96-98 Trajan 98-117	Vologases I 51-80 Parthian War with Rome 53-63 Osroes (Chosroes) 89-128
100 AD **135 AD**	Jewish uprisings in Palestine, Egypt, Mesopotamia 116-117 Bar-Kochba Revolt 132-135 Jerusalem razed, Aelia Capitolina built on site	Campaigns in Dacia 101-107 Hadrian 117-138	Conquest of Nabateans by Romans Trajan invades Parthia 114 Territory lost to Romans regained 118

Herod and His Descendants

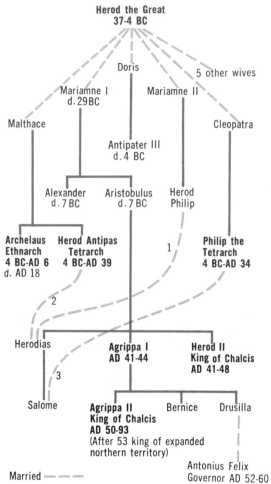

Married — — — —

1. First marriage of Herodias.
2. Second marriage of Herodias.
3. Salome, daughter of Herodias and Herod (sometimes referred to as Philip), danced before Herod Antipas for John the Baptist's head. She married her great-uncle Philip the Tetrarch.

d. died

Roman catapult. A type of artillery used effectively by both Romans and Jews in the battle for Jerusalem, A.D. 69-70.

Gazetteer-Index

This Gazetteer-Index is an alphabetical listing of all geographical names found on the maps of this volume. The spelling of Biblical names used on maps and index is that found in the Revised Standard Version (RSV). Alternative Biblical or other ancient names are given in parentheses. Wherever possible, the modern equivalent (Arabic, Hebrew, Turkish, etc.) of an ancient name is given in italic type. A question mark after the identification of a site indicates that the location is possible or probable but not yet certain. The page numbers of the maps on which the name appears are listed in sequence. The key or grid reference (a letter-figure combination) following the page number(s) refers to the letters and figures at the margins of the maps. For example, Azotus (Ashdod in Old Testament times) [Arabic *Isdud*, Hebrew *Tel Ashdod*] can be found on the maps on pages 23, 25, 26 and 35 at key reference W6 and on page 31 at G8. Entries for locations within or near Jerusalem give the page numbers only for the appropriate Jerusalem maps.

ABBREVIATIONS

T. = Tell, Tel (mound)
Kh. = Khirbet (ruin)
H. = Horvat (ruin)
J. = Jebel (hill or mount)
W. = Wadi (seasonal stream)

A

Abana, *Nahr Barada,* river. 4:Z2
Abel, (Abel-beth-maachah), *T. Abil.* 12, 14, 15:Y3; 13:H5
Abel-meholah, *Kh. el-Maqlub.* 15:Y4
Abila, *T. Abil,* in Decapolis. 23, 25, 26, 27, 28:Y4
Abila, *T. Abila,* in Abilene. 25, 26:Z2
Abilene, region. 25, 26:X2; 31:H6
Abū Rudays. 39:C6
Abū Zanimah. 39:C6
Abydos, *Arabet el-Madfuneh,* in Egypt. 9, 16:F6
Abydos, *Canakkale,* in Asia Minor. 16:E2
Accaron, *see* Ekron
Acco, (Ptolemais, Acre), *'Akko, T. el-Fukhkhar.* 4, 11, 12, 14, 15, 19, 23, 38:X3; 8:B4; 10:D2; 13:G5
Accrabbah, (Akrabatta), *'Aqraba.* 19:X5
Achaean League. 21, 22:C1
Achaia, Roman province. 32, 33:A1; 36:F3
Achmetha, *see* Ecbatana
Achzib, (Ecdippa), *es-Zib.* 11, 12, 19, 38:X3
Achzib-Acco, region. 19:X3
Acra, in Jerusalem. 22
Adasa, *Kh. 'Addasa.* 23:X6
Adida, (Hadid), *el-Haditheh.* 23, 35:W5
Adora, (Adoraim), *Dura.* 23, 25:W6
Adoraim, (Adora), *Dura.* 12, 15:W6
Adramyttium, *Edremit.* 32, 33:B1; 33:C4
Adria, (Adriatic Sea). 33:A4
Adullam, *T. esh-Sheikh Madhkur.* 11, 12, 15, 19, 23:X6
Aegean Sea. 17, 20, 32, 33:A1
Aenon, spring north of *Kh. Umm el-'Umdan* (?). 26:X5
Aetolian League. 21, 22:C1
Africa, Roman province. 36:C4
'Afula. 39:D3
Agade, *Abu Ghubar* (?). 9:J4
Agrippias, (Anthedon), *el-Blahiyeh.* 25,26:V6
Agrippina, *Kaukab el-Hawa.* 26, 27:X4
Ahlab, *Kh. el-Mahalib.* 11:X3
Ai, *et-Tell.* 8:B6; 10:E3; 11, 12, 19, 38:X6
Aijalon, *Yalo.* 11, 12, 15:X6
Aijalon, Valley of, *W. Selman.* 4, 11, 12:W6
'Ain Feshkha, spring. 34, 38:X6

'Ain Gedi, (En-gedi). 34, 38:X7
'Ain Karim, (Beth-haccherem). 38:X6
'Ajlūn. 39:E3
Akhetaton, *Tell el-Amarna.* 8:E5; 10:A7
Akkad, region. 9:J4
'Akko, (Acco, Ptolemais). 39:D2
Akrabatta, (Accrabbah), *'Aqraba.* 35:X5
Akrabattene, region. 23:X8
Akrabbim, Ascent of, *Naqb es-Safa.* 15:X8
Alaca Huyuk. 9:G1
Alalakh. 9:G3
Al 'Aqabah. 39:D5
Al 'Arish. 39:C4
Alashiya, (Cyprus). 9:F3
Aleppo, (Haleb), *Halab.* 16:G3
Alexandria, *Alexandretta,* in Syria. 31:H2
Alexandria, *Gulashkird,* in Carmania. 20:E4
Alexandria, *Iskandariyeh,* in Egypt. 20, 23, 21, 22:D2; 33:66; 37:G5; *see also city plan p. 21*
Alexandria Arachosiorum, *Ghazni.* 20:F3
Alexandria Ariou, *Herat.* 20:F3
Alexandria Eschata, *Khodzent.* 21:G2
Alexandrium, *Qarn Sartabeh.* 23, 25, 26:X5
Al Fayyūm. 39:A6
Al Firdān. 39:B4
Al Harmal. 39:E1
Al Karak. 39:E4
Al Khalil, (Hebron). 34:X6
Al Khuraybah. 39:D7
Al Kuntillah. 39:D5
Al Mafraq. 39:E3
Al Mahallah al Kubra. 39:A4
Al Manṣurāh. 39:A4
Al Minyā. 39:A7
Al Mudawwarah. 39:E6
Al Qāhirah, (Cairo). 39:A5
Al Qantarah. 39:B4
Al Qatrānah. 39:E4
Al Qunaytirah. 39:E2
Al Qusaymah. 39:D4
Alush, *Wadi el-Esh* (?). 10:C6
Amalek, Amalekites, people. 12:X6; 13:G7; 14:W8
Amanus Mts. 31:H2
Amarna, Tell el-, (Akhetaton). 10, 39:A7
Amastris. 37:G3
Amathus, *T. 'Ammata.* 23, 25, 26:Y5
Amisus. 37:H3
Amman, (Rabba, Philadelphia). 38:Y5; 39:E3
Ammon, region. 4, 11, 12, 14, 15, 19:Z5; 8:C5; 10:E3; 13:H6; 16:G4

Amon, Temple of, *Siwa.* 18, 20:A3
Amorites, people. 8:B6
Amphipolis, *Neochori.* 32, 33:A1
Anab, *Kh. 'Anab es-Saghireh.* 12:W6
Anat, *'Anah.* 16:H4; 17:C3
Anathoth, *Ras el-Kharrubeh.* 12, 19:X6
Anchialus. 37:G3
Ancyra, *Ankara.* 16:F2; 18, 20:B2; 32, 33:C1; 37:G3
Ankuwa, *Alisar Huyuk.* 9:G2
An Nakhl. 39:C5
Anthedon, (Agrippias), *el-Blahiyeh.* 23, 25:V6
Anti-Lebanon, mts. 4:Y2; 8:C2; 31:J5
Antioch, *Antakya,* in Syria. 22:D1; 31:H3; 32, 33:D2; 37:H4; *see also city plan p. 30*
Antioch, *Yalvac,* in Pisidia. 32:C1; 32:C2; 37:G3
Antipatris, (Aphek), *Ras el-'Ain.* 25, 26, 28, 35, 38:W5
Antium, *Anzio.* 36:D3
Antonia Fortress, in Jerusalem. 25, 29, 34
Apamea, *Qal'at el-Mudiq.* 31, 37:H4
Aphairema, (Ephraim, Ophrah), *et-Taiyibeh* (?). 23:X5
Aphek, (Antipatris), *Ras el-'Ain.* 10:D3; 11, 12, 14, 15, 38:X5
Aphek, *Fiq,* in Transjordan. 15:Y4
Aphek, *T. Kurdaneh,* in Asher. 11, 12:X3
Apollonia, *Arsuf,* in Palestine. 19, 23, 25, 26, 35:W5
Apollonia, *Pollinia,* in Macedonia. 32, 33:A1
Apollonia, *Sozopol,* on Black Sea. 18:B1
Appius, Forum of, (Appi Forum). 33:A4
Aqaba, Gulf of. 10, 39:D6
Ar, *el-Misna'.* 14, 15:Y7
Arabah, *el- Ghor, Wadi al 'Arabah.* 4, 15:X8; 10:D5; 13:H8; 39:E4
Arabia, region. 9:H5; 18, 20:C3; 21, 22:E2; 37:J5
Arabian Sea. 21:F4
Arabs, people. 16:H5; 17:C3
Arachosia, region. 18, 20:F3
Arad, *T. 'Arad.* 8:B7; 10:D4; 11, 12, 14, 15, 23, 34:X7; 13:G6; 39:D3
Aral Sea. 17, 18, 20:E1
Aram, (Syria), region. 14, 15:Y2
Aram-Damascus, region. 13:H4
Arameans, people. 11:Y2
Aram-zobah, region. 13:J4
Araq, el-Emir, (Tyrus). 38:Y6

Ararat, (Urartu), region. 16:H2
Ararat, Mt., *Buyuk Agri Dagi.* 9, 16:J2
Araxes, river. 9:K2; 16:J2; 18:D1
Arbela, *Erbil,* in Assyria. 9, 16:J3; 18, 20:D2
Arbela, *Irbid,* in Decapolis. 26:Y4
Arbela, *Kh. Irbid,* in Galilee. 23:X4
Archelais, *Kh. 'Auja et-Tahta.* 26:X5
Ardus, (Arvad), *Erwad, Ruwad.* 31:H4
Areopolis, (Rabbath-moab), *Kh. er-Rabba.* 26, 28:Y7
Argob, region. 13:H5; 14:Y3
Aria, region. 18, 21:F3
Aribi, (Arabs), people. 16:H4
Ariha, (Jericho). 34:X6
Arimathea, (Ramathaim), *Rentis.* 26:X5
'Arish, Wadi al-, (River of Egypt). 4, V8; 39:C3
Armenia, region. 18, 20:C2; 21, 22:E1; 37:J3
Arnon, W. al-Mawjib, river. 4, 11, 12, 14, 15, 19, 23, 25, 26, 35:Y7; 8:B6; 10:E4
Aroer, *'Ara'ir,* in Moab. 11, 12.Y6; 13:H6
Arpad, *T. Erfad.* 16:G3
Arvad, (Ardus), *Erwad, Ruwad.* 9, 16:G3; 13:H3; 18:C3; 31:H4
Arzawa, region. 8:E2
Ascalon, (Ashkelon), *'Ashqelon.* 23, 25, 26, 35, 38:W6
Ashdod, (Azotus), *Isdud, T. Ashdod.* 8:A6; 11, 12, 14, 15, 19, 23, 38:W6; 10, 39:D3
Ashdod, region. 19:W6
Asher, tribe. 11, 12:X3
Ashkelon, (Ascalon), *'Ashqelon.* 8:A6; 10:D3; 11, 12, 14, 15, 19, 23:W6; 13:G6
'Ashqelon. 39:D3
Ashtaroth, *T. 'Ashtarah.* 8:C4; 10:E2; 11, 12, 14, 15:Y4; 13:H5
Asia, Roman province. 32, 33:B1; 33:C5; 37:G3
Asia Minor, region. 20:B2
Asochis, *Kh. el-Lon.* 26, 27:X4
Asphaltitis, Lake, (Dead Sea). 25, 26, 35:X6
As Salṭ. 39:E3
As Samu', (Eshtemoa). 34:X7
Asshur, *Qal'at Sherqat.* 9:J3; 16:J3; 18:C2
Assuwa, region. 8:E1
Assyria, region. 9:J3; 16:H3; 17:C2
Assyrian Empire. 16:G4
Astacus. 16:F2
Astorga. 36:A2
Ataroth, *Kh. Attarus.* 15:Y6

Picture Credits

The editor and publisher wish to express their thanks and appreciation to the following for supplying illustrations:

The American Numismatic Society, New York: pages 20 (bottom), 21 (top right), 22 (center left), 28 (bottom right), 29 (bottom left), 35 (bottom). Henry Angelo-Castrillon: page 32 (top right), 36 (right). The Bettmann Archive, New York: page 42. The Trustees of the British Museum: pages 16 (all three photos), 18 (top). The Brooklyn Museum, Charles Edwin Wilbour Fund: page 37 (top right). Ernest J. Dupuy: pages 32 (top left), 36 (center), 37 (center). GAF Pana-Vue Slides: pages 24 (top), 28 (top). Hebrew University, Jerusalem, Department of Archaeology: page 22 (bottom right). Iran National Tourist Office, New York: page 18 (left). Israel Government Tourist Office, New York: title page, pages 5 (bottom left), 11 (two photos at top), 27 (left), 29 (top left), 30 (second from top), 34 (center left), 35 (center left). The Israel Museum, Jerusalem: pages 14 (top right), 18 (bottom right), 28 (bottom left). Istanbul Museum: page 30 (top). Italian Government Travel Office: page 36 (left). Nancy L. Lapp: page 12. From Lepsius, *Denkmaeler:* page 10 (right). Herbert G. May: page 27 (bottom right). The Metropolitan Museum of Art: pages 2, 22 (top left and top right), 37 (bottom right). Museo Nazionale, Naples: pages 20 (top), 21 (center right). Museum of Fine Arts, Boston: page 24 (bottom). Notre Dame de Sion, Jerusalem: page 29 (center bottom). The Oriental Institute, University of Chicago: pages 17, 38 (center). William L. Reed, courtesy American Schools of Oriental Research: page 35 (top). The University Museum, University of Pennsylvania: pages 9, 37 (left). Wide World Photos: page 30 (third from top).

Photographs from collection of Professor Harry Thomas Frank: pages 5 (three photos at right), 7 (both), 8, 10 (left), 11 (bottom), 14 (top left), 21 (top left), 22 (center right and bottom left), 25, 27 (center and top right), 29 (center top and right), 30 (bottom), 32 (bottom), 34 (top), 38 (top and four bottom photos).